Shortcuts

for
TEACHING LANGUAGE USAGE

Activities for Punctuation, Capitalization, Grammar, and Usage

By Flora Joy

Illustrated by Pat Harroll

Cover by Janet Skiles

Copyright © 1994, Good Apple

ISBN No. 0-86653-805-4

Printing No. 98765

Good Apple, Inc.
299 Jefferson Road
P.O. Box 480
Parsippany, NJ 07054-0480

Paramount Publishing

Dedicated to Pam Johnson

TABLE OF CONTENTS

Language Mechanics
and
Whole Language

A major misconception of many teachers who are initially learning about the whole language philosophy of teaching is that *skills are not taught* in whole language classrooms. This is not only untrue, but it is also a dangerous error. Although whole language classrooms are not organized by a set number of minutes for each separate, isolated skill (thank goodness!), the skills are a very important and integral part of any effectively planned whole language program!

The skills of language mechanics are among the toughest to teach. Traditional methods of teaching these skills have involved the much-dreaded sterile ditto pages that have little to do with real life. Some clever students become adept at bypassing their brains while filling out such pages. The intent of this book, therefore, is to present an approach to language mechanics in a format that will "stick to the brain." These activities involve a fun element for classroom interaction and language mastery. They complement any textbook series, any workbook series, and any teaching approach—including all whole language philosophies.

Users of this material are requested to incorporate these activities with their current language arts program. If a class is reading *Charlotte's Web*, for example, a sentence could be written about Charlotte or Wilbur that contains the items twirled in the Sentence Wheel activity. All activities can be correlated with literature selections.

Teachers are limited only to their own imaginations regarding the incorporation of these activities into their regular academic setting. Language mechanics skills *must* be taught. Why not, therefore, teach them in a fun and exciting manner?

GA1497

Activities
for
ALL
AREAS

GA1497

The majority of the activities in this book are designed for one of the skill areas: punctuation, capitalization, grammar, or usage. This section, however, encompasses activities that involve more than one of these language tasks, and it provides explanations of activities (such as the Pop-Up activities) that are developed in each of the four subsequent sections.

Pop-Up Activities

Pop-up activities are a major part of this collection of teaching tools. They appear in all sections of this book. Therefore, to save space, one general explanation is given for all. Each separate activity will additionally have its own specific information in a later section.

Concept of Pop-Up Activities:

The concept of the pop-up activities is for the student to "pop up" the right answer. These answers will be shown when students hold up cards corresponding to the correct answers. Several different pop-up card sets for a variety of different skills are included in this book.

Classroom Procedures:

The specific directions may differ from one set of pop-up cards to another, but the following will generally apply:

Give each student a set of pop-up cards. The cards in these sets are generally all placed in full view on the tops of the students' desks.

Read an item that will have an answer on one and only one of these cards. Use any wording you wish. The following is an example: "You have four cards on your desk. One has the word *noun*, one *pronoun*, one *verb*, and one *adjective*. We have studied these four parts of speech, and we are now going to do a fun activity with them. I will ask you a question that has an answer of *noun, pronoun, verb,* or *adjective*. You will decide which one it is and then hold up that card. Do not say your answer aloud; just hold up the card you think is right." After the students understand these directions, you are then ready to proceed with your prepared questions. For example, you may ask, "What part of speech is the word *run* in the sentence *She has a run in her hose?*"

Students (silently) hold up the appropriate card after they have carefully thought through the answer. Those with the correct answer will be holding up the **noun** card.

GA1497

You can tell at a glance who has the correct answers, and you may discuss the questions if several students have incorrect responses.

Always follow each question by saying, "The correct answer is (??)." **NEVER** call attention to someone who does not have a correct answer! It is very critical for students to know *they will not be embarrassed* if they hold up the wrong card. Classrooms are for **learning**. We all learn through our errors. Mistakes should not only be allowed, but they should provide the opportunity to point out the needed direction of future instruction. Don't even frown or grimace at a student holding an incorrect card. (Yes, I know that isn't always possible!)

By always saying, "The correct answer is (??)" before going to the next question, you can help students know immediately if their card choices are right or wrong. When several students are incorrect, you have some choices before revealing the right answer. One is to give a response such as "Think about this for a minute. The word *run* **is** very often a verb, but is it a verb in this sentence? Do any of you want to change your minds?" Another response might be, "A different word I could use in this sentence in the place of *run* is *flaw*. If the sentence were *She has a flaw in her hose*, what would the part of speech of the word *flaw* be?" A very different response might be "The word *run* is used as the direct object in this sentence. The direct object is one of two parts of speech. Are you holding up one of these two?" Any type of teaching dialog that fits the occasion will be appropriate at this point. Stop at any time to teach or reteach any skill.

For a question that is missed by several students and discussed afterwards, ask that same question a few minutes later to see if the concept has finally been grasped. This method will help you plan future concepts to be taught and the degree of emphasis to place on them.

As you continue with questions centering around a specific skill, make mental notes of those students who do not seem to have grasped the concept. These students may later be pulled aside for further instruction or activities while those who demonstrated adequate knowledge can proceed to new material. This procedure allows for individual challenges in academic material rather than having everyone enrolled in the same grade or class work on the same page at the same time simply because it is presented that way in the curriculum guide!

Student Benefits:

There are numerous benefits (as described by the students themselves) of using pop-up cards. The following are selected ones:

There is no writing to do! (Yeah!)

They are fun. I like them three trillion times better than those ditto pages!

I'm not embarrassed when I make a mistake. I am the only one who knows about it unless I make a dumb remark out loud.

I know immediately if my answer is right or wrong. I don't have to wait until my paper is returned the next day or the next week after I have already forgotten what the questions were.

The class period passes so fast!

Teacher Benefits:

Teachers have also explained the advantages as they see them. Here are a few from teachers who have used these cards repeatedly:

There are no papers to grade! (Yeah!) One word-for-word teacher's comment is as follows: Have you ever graded pages of punctuation marks that looked like the floor plan of a Siberian jungle? When I finish, they look like a *bloody* floor plan of a Siberian jungle! I have marked all over the place and I feel as if I have gotten nowhere. When I give the papers back, I get the "so-what" response. With these pop-up cards I can **see** if students are understanding this relatively complex part of written language without taking home hours of thankless paper-grading tasks.

The greatest advantage of all is that **every student must respond to <u>every</u> question <u>every</u> time**. Whenever I have a prepared list of oral questions for review, for example, no matter how absolutely wonderful they might be, only one student can answer one question at a time. If I have thirty questions and thirty students, each student will, on the average, be able to answer only one question. The remaining students just sit there and are simply not active in the learning process. After they have answered their "one question," they can actually go to sleep with their eyes open. Nobody, however, can sleep while using pop-up cards!

I can see progress (or lack of it) immediately. Sometimes I think I have done a terrific job teaching a skill—only to learn that the students have been giving me that "knowing nod" while they were daydreaming.

I know which students need supplementary work. Not everybody needs to do the 8,791 workbook pages on capital letters. Therefore, I make a mental note of those who missed several items and give the extra instruction and attention specifically to those individuals. The rest of my students are not wasting time with instruction on a topic in which they are already knowledgeable.

These cards are tremendous for pretesting. About a week before I plan a unit on a topic (such as simple subjects and predicates), I will use these cards to help me decide the amount of planning I need to do.

I use these cards immediately before achievement tests. I know the concepts covered on these tests, and I want this information to be present in my students' minds while they are taking these tests. Pop-up cards provide a great review.

These cards always help me at the end of a unit before I give the unit quiz. I tell the students to let their pop-up answers help them decide how much and in what areas they need to study.

Pop-up cards are great to use when evaluators visit my classroom. I give additional sets of cards to these visitors and ask them to respond also. As a result they more frequently seem to appreciate what I am trying to teach.

Added Thoughts:

What about competition with these cards? These cards should generally not be used in a competitive way. Learning should occur at each individual's own rate rather than at competitive speed. Try to allow a reasonable amount of time for these responses.

What about "cheating"? It is possible even with traditional classroom seating for a student's peripheral vision to pick up the answer held by an adjacent classmate. However, you can usually tell when this is happening. I never call attention to this issue; I simply treat it as if a student has given an incorrect answer. Students who are secure in their knowledge will usually hold up their pop-up cards with confidence. Sometimes students will hold up a card, then look around to see if others are holding up the same answer. If not, they will sometimes make a sudden switch. I also make a mental note that "Sally" was not giving correct answers. In circular seating or some other classroom arrangement where students' cards are easily seen by others, I ask that all look at their own cards until they have made a choice. After they have their cards in the air, then I tell them they are free to look at the cards of others. Note that when cards can easily be seen by others, students may be more readily embarrassed with their inappropriate answers.

GA1497

How often should I use these cards? Because the sets of cards are different, it is possible to use them with relative frequency. As with any activity, cease its use before the interest wanes.

Can I make cards not provided in this book? The sky is the limit! Go for it!

Preparation Instructions:

There are many ways to prepare pop-up cards. The following is one suggested way:

Photocopy the pages of cards onto stiff, colorful paper. If your school's copiers cannot accommodate stiff paper, investigate the commercial printers in your area.

Make as many sets as you will need at one time. For example, if you have thirty students and plan to use the cards for whole-group instruction, it would be wise to make thirty sets of cards. (Remember, they are reusable for 3,048 years!)

For organizational purposes, number these card sets before you cut the pages. On each card is the word *Set*. In the brief blank space following that word, write the same number on each card that will be in that set. (I promise you that you will later be glad you did this.) This step is important in case you do not have perfect students. For example, if you have used thirty sets of punctuation cards (Set 1, Set 2, Set 3 . . . Set 30), and after the activity has been completed you find a question-mark card on the floor with Set 12 written on it, you will not need to look through thirty envelopes to see which one is missing a question-mark card. Just find envelope 12.

An optional step is to write or stamp your name or the name of your school on the backs of all cards.

Another optional step is to laminate these pages or cover them with clear self-adhesive paper, thus making these cards more durable.

Cut out the cards in each set. Place all Set 1 cards in an envelope and write Set 1 on the outside of that envelope. Do the same for Set 2, Set 3, etc.

File all labeled envelopes together in a large container. These are now ready for student use—and there will be no future preparation (unless a card is lost, etc.).

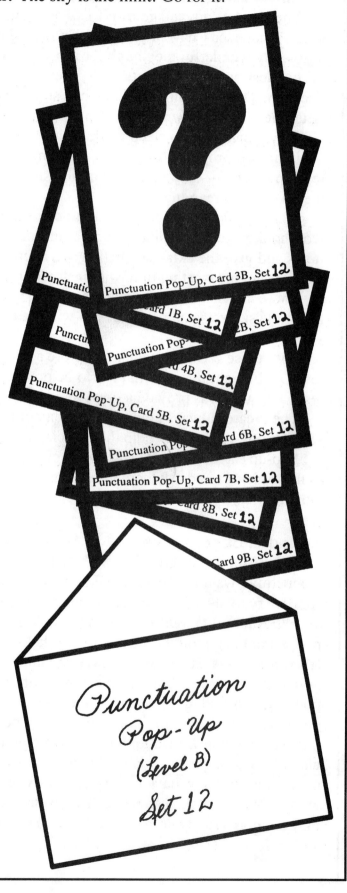

GA1497

Fill-In Fun Activities

A special type of exercise for teaching punctuation, capitalization, grammar, and usage is called Fill-In Fun. These activities may be designed for any one or all of these skills. Following this explanation are several examples of Fill-In Fun activities that combine two or more of these skills.

The Fill-In Fun activities provide learners with a page of text with ten to fifty blanks. For each blank space students will be thinking through a specific language concept and writing a response on the provided line. Each page has the specific skill(s) indicated on the top line, followed by the actual number of blank spaces to be completed on that page. Student instructions follow, although these directions may need to be read to younger learners.

Classroom Procedures: There are several ways to use these pages with students.

The traditional method: This method has each student completing each page independently.

Small-group arrangements: When appropriate, groups of two to four could complete the pages with discussion occurring as needed. Note that more than four in such a group often results in having one or two who do not contribute significantly to the final page completion. The group that finishes with the highest number of correct answers within a predetermined time limit could be recognized in a positive fashion.

Transparency presentation: Several transparency presentation methods could be used. (Be sure the quality of the transparency allows an adequate view of symbols such as punctuation marks.) The transparency could be used either for instruction or for checking answers.

Big-book style: The sheets in this book may be enlarged and presented to a small group for discussion. If these large pages are laminated, a grease pencil (or some crayons) may be used to mark the responses, thus allowing the large pages to be reusable. A variety of clever challenges may be proposed. For example, markers (of four different colors) may be given to each person in a four-member group. Individuals may take turns marking the items. After the page has been completed, then it is checked. The color with the highest number of correct items is the "winner." Several variations on this idea could be successfully implemented.

Difficulty Range: There is no such thing as a "third-grade skill." Skills in language mechanics are lifetime problems for most speakers and writers. Therefore, assigning a grade level to these pages is impossible. However, the appearance and number of blanks will help determine the level of use. Should you encounter a page appropriate for your classroom but with a few items too difficult, consider filling in the answers for these items before photocopying the exercise. In this manner the students are at least seeing appropriate responses prior to their formal introduction of those skills in the classroom.

Scoring and Checking: These pages are primarily intended to be used to promote language learning and discussion. If scores are to be given, the number of items per page may be used to calculate the point credit for each item. Methods of checking student work will differ according to the skill featured on each page. Usage Fill-In Fun, for example, can be checked by reading the passage aloud. Those involving skills such as capitalization, however, will need to be checked in a different manner.

GA1497

Preparation of Future Fill-In Fun Pages: Pages such as those provided may be prepared for additional exercises in any of these language areas. Do consider attempting to make the page attractive by using some type of character or picture. These illustrations may be found in a variety of sources:

- Coloring books
- Magazines and newspapers
- Photos of **you**
- Computer graphics

The majority of the graphics provided in this book came from the computer graphics program CorelDRAW! They were modified for these Fill-In Fun pages. CorelDRAW! is a graphic arts corporation located in Canada (1600 Carling Avenue, Ottawa, Ontario, Canada KIZ8R7).

One method of preparation involves pasting the graphic on the page, then using the remaining space for the text and blanks. If your textbooks or workbooks have interesting material for these skills, consider using them (with possible alterations) for these fill-in activities. Otherwise you may prepare your own original material. If so, do not expect to produce a literary masterpiece; the need to use selected words repeatedly (such as *lie* and *lay*) combined with the limited space factor will almost surely result in a brief, silly narrative. Most students, however, find this amusing and prefer this format to the more traditional methods of material presentation.

Samples Provided for General Skills: On the following pages, there are two samples of Fill-In Fun activities that allow for a combination of general language mechanics learning. The first ("The Jogger") is a very simple exercise for choosing between *ran* and *run* and selecting the appropriate end punctuation for sentences. The second ("The Day My Mother Was Angry") offers a challenge to practically any student in pre-high school years. Some of the fifty choices are relatively simple, but most require learners to think through a mechanical language skill.

With this or any other material for language mechanics, always remember to cease the activity while learners are still excited about it! Keep them wanting more!

Answers for Pages 13 and 14:

"The Jogger": Late each day when it's really dark, a jogger runs by my house. He has run every night for two weeks. Yesterday he ran around our block seven times. I wonder why he has run so long on our street. The third time he ran by, I became frightened. Would this man hurt me? Should I call the police?

Suddenly our front door opened. The jogger ran inside our house.

"Yikes!" I screamed in a very loud voice.

Then I looked at the jogger, who by then had run out of breath.

The jogger was my dad.

"The Day My Mother Was Angry": On July 7, 1996, seven of my cousins came to visit me from New Jersey. They always spend a few weeks with me each summer in the country instead of going to Camp Imaloozer. One day around 3:00 Tommy, my youngest cousin, saw a chameleon while we were hiking near Stone Mountain.

"Wow!" said Frank, his brother. "It must have been lying there for a long time because it's the same color as the rock."

"Oh, nonsense," protested Julie, the older of the two girls who were with us. "Don't chameleons usually turn the color of whatever they're sitting on?"

"I know what let's do," suggested Wanda as she whispered her plan to us.

When my cousins and I returned home, Mom was lying down; therefore, we put our plan to work. Later we heard a terrible scream! Charlie had set the chameleon on Mom's dress. Because of its identical color she didn't see it until she sat up. Until that day I didn't know my mom had such lungs!

Fill-In Fun: Run/Ran and End Punctuation (12) Name: _____

The Jogger

Late each day when it's really dark, a jogger runs by my house.

He has _____ every night for two weeks_ Yesterday he
(ran run)   (. ?)

_____ around our
(ran run)

block seven times. I

wonder why he has

_____ so long on our
(ran run)

street_ The third time he
(. ?)

_____ by, I became
(ran run)

frightened. Would this

man hurt me_ Should I
(. ?)

call the police_
(. ?)

   Suddenly our front door

opened. The jogger

_____ inside our
(ran run)

house.

   "Yikes_" I screamed in
(! .)

a very loud voice_
(! .)

   Then I looked at the

jogger, who by then had

_____ out of breath.
(ran run)

The jogger was my dad.

GA1497

Student Instructions: In each blank space write a word, a letter, or a mark of punctuation—choosing <u>only</u> from one of the items in parentheses immediately below the blank. When only one choice is provided, you may either write that item in the blank or you may write nothing at all if no punctuation is needed in that spot. There is only one correct answer for each blank.

The __ay My Mother __as __ngry
(D d)   (W w) (A a)

On __uly_ 7_ 1996_ seven of my __ousins came to visit me from
(J j) (,) (,) (, ;) (C c)

__ew __ersey. They always spend a few weeks with me each
(N n) (J j)

__ummer in the __ountry instead of going to __amp Imaloozer. One
(S s) (C c) (C c)

day around 3_00 Tommy_ my youngest __ousin, _____ a
(. :) (,) (C c) (saw seen)

chameleon while we were hiking near __tone __ountain.
(S s) (M m)

Wow" said Frank_ his brother_ "It must
(") (. !) (,) (. ")

have been _____ there for a long time
(laying lying)

because _____ the same color as the rock._
(its it's) (! ")

_Oh_ nonsense_" protested Julie_ the
(") (, ;) (, ?) (,)

_____ of the two girls who were with us.
(older oldest)

"_____ chameleons usually turn the
(Don't Doesn't)

color of whatever _____ sitting on_"
(there they're their) (. ?)

"I _____ what let_s do," suggested
(know no) (')

Wanda as she whispered her plan to us_
(" .)

When my cousins and ___ returned home_
(I me) (,)

Mom was _____ down_ therefore, we put
(lying laying) (, ;)

our plan _____ work. Later we heard a terrible
(to two too)

scream_ Charlie had _____ the chameleon on
(? !) (set sat)

Mom_s dress. Because of ____ identical color
(') (its it's)

she didn_t see it until she _____ up. Until
(') (set sat)

that day I didn't _____ my __om had
(know no) (M m)

such lungs!

14

GA1497

Activities
for
Teaching
PUNCTUATION

GA1497

Punctuation is a skill needed by writers only. Speakers "punctuate" their talk using techniques such as vocal pausing. Writers, on the other hand, need to use specially designed visual symbols. Knowing how, when, and where to place these symbols can be taught in fun and exciting ways, but these marks must be _seen_ during the learning process. Here are some unusual and different activities for helping young learners deal with punctuation.

GA1497

Punctuation Probe

Learners should be actively involved in the process of deciding where punctuation marks should be placed. Punctuation Probe provides an opportunity for such participation.

Preparation Instructions:

Photocopy those large punctuation marks on pages 20-27 that pertain to the current language needs of your students. Second graders, for example, may not yet need to use the semicolon or the colon. Make extra copies of frequently used marks such as the period and comma. Trim these marks close to the edge, being careful with the question mark, exclamation mark, colon, and semicolon to leave them as one mark. Glue these trimmed marks onto stiff paper. Trim the stiff paper, leaving about a one-inch (2.5 cm) border on all sides. Optional: Cover these pieces with a clear, self-adhesive film or paper for permanent use.

If an overhead projector will be used, prepare the punctuation marks transparency as shown on page 19.

Classroom Procedures:

Prepare sentences that the learners would need to punctuate. These may be sentences from the language arts textbook for your class or from any other available language arts textbooks or language workbooks.

Place the prepared punctuation marks on a table near the front of the classroom.

Use one of the following methods for sentence viewing:

- Chalkboard Punctuation Probe: Write one sentence on the chalkboard, leaving out the punctuation marks. (See illustration on page 18.)

- Punctuation Probe with Word Cards: Write the individual words of the sentence onto separate word cards. Number the backs of these word cards for ease in student use. If possible, prepare each separate sentence in a different color or label the sentences in a fashion for organizational purposes. (See illustration on page 18.)

- Punctuation Probe with an Overhead Projector: Write the sentences on a sheet of acetate or a blank transparency. Leave spaces for the later inclusion of the punctuation marks. See page 19 for a sheet of transparency images for this method. An illustration of this method is shown on page 18.

Present the sentence to be punctuated. Have several designated students go to the punctuation table and select one mark of punctuation to hold in its appropriate place in the sentence.

Have remaining class members determine if the sentence is accurately punctuated. Any necessary revision or discussion may occur. (Note the difference in the students' responses to this active exercise as opposed to completing a work sheet!)

After several demonstration sentences have been used, the learners may create sentences to be used with this activity. They should be encouraged to write sentences that will require more than end punctuation. This will help students review the use of these other punctuation marks. For the added value of peer tutoring, this step may occur in small groups of three to six students. A selected group member could write the next sentence for the entire class to punctuate.

GA1497

Illustration of Chalkboard Punctuation Probe

Illustration of Punctuation Probe with Word Cards

Illustration of Punctuation Probe
with Overhead Projector

18

GA1497

Punctuation Probe with the Overhead Projector

For punctuation marks to be used with an overhead projector, make a transparency of this page. Cut out each punctuation mark just inside the dotted lines so the dotted lines will not show. The space below each punctuation mark will allow a "gripper" for students to grasp the mark. Two extra periods and commas are provided. If you plan to use sentences having more of these marks, then prepare an extra page of marks. An optional extra challenge may be issued with the hyphen, dash, parentheses, and single quotation marks. These may be omitted for younger learners.

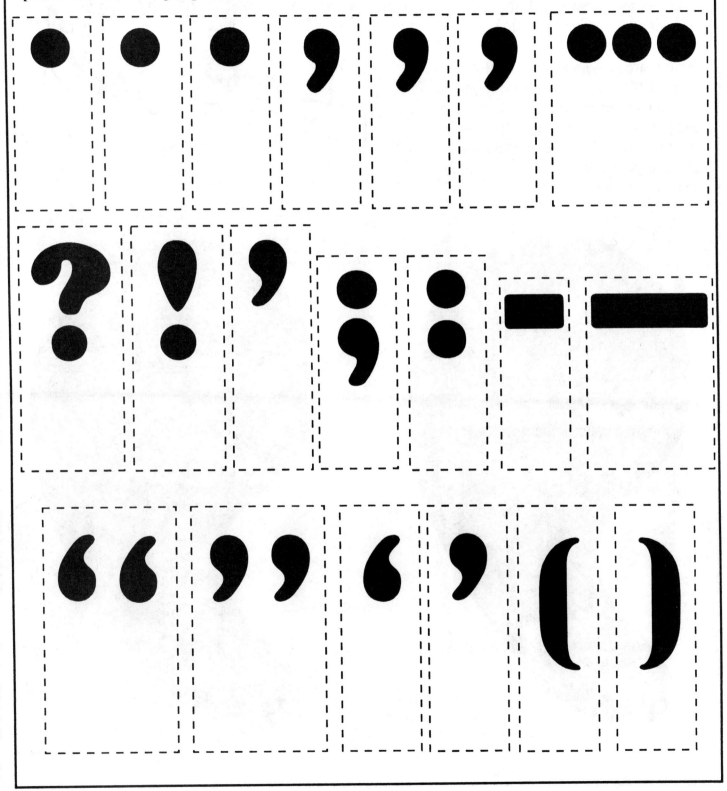

GA1497

Large Marks for Punctuation Probe

The two punctuation marks below and the marks on the following seven pages may be used for Punctuation Probe when the entire class will be viewing the sentences. If your prepared sentences will contain more than two (total) commas and apostrophes, prepare an extra set of those shown at the bottom of this page. A total of four periods are provided because of the extra possible uses with abbreviations inside sentences in addition to the final end punctuation mark. The illustrations at the right show the preparation of these large marks. Modify this in any desired manner.

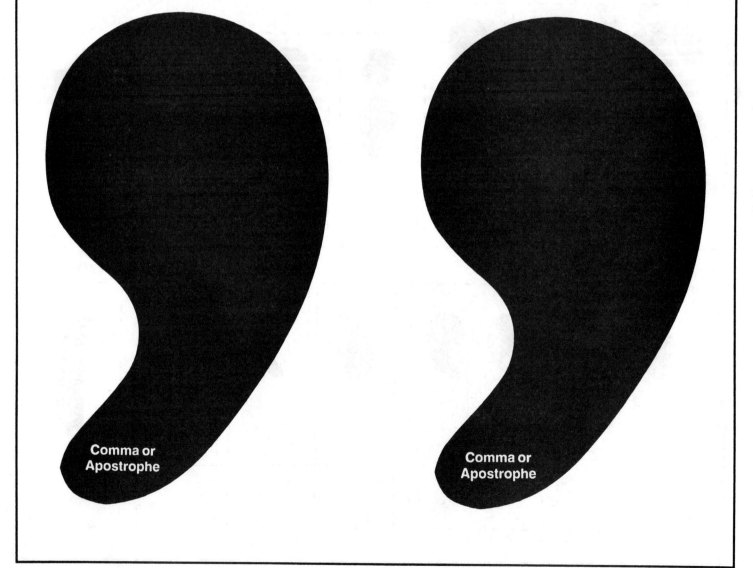

Comma or Apostrophe

Comma or Apostrophe

GA1497

**Large Marks for
Punctuation Probe
(Question Mark)**

**Question
Mark**

21

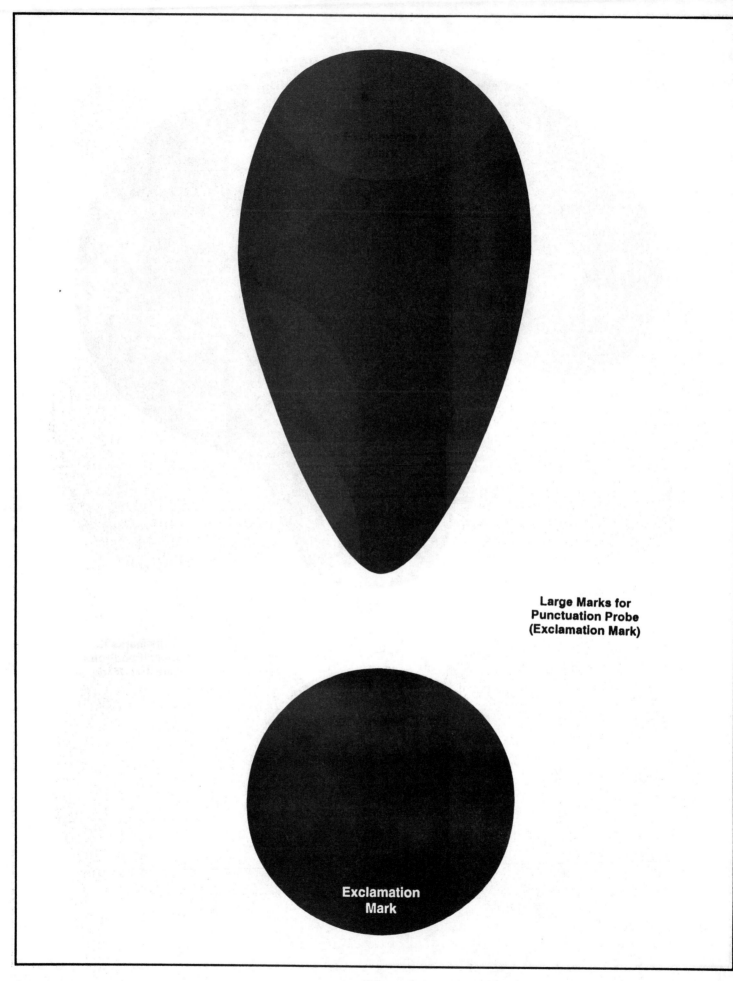

**Large Marks for
Punctuation Probe
(Exclamation Mark)**

**Exclamation
Mark**

GA1497

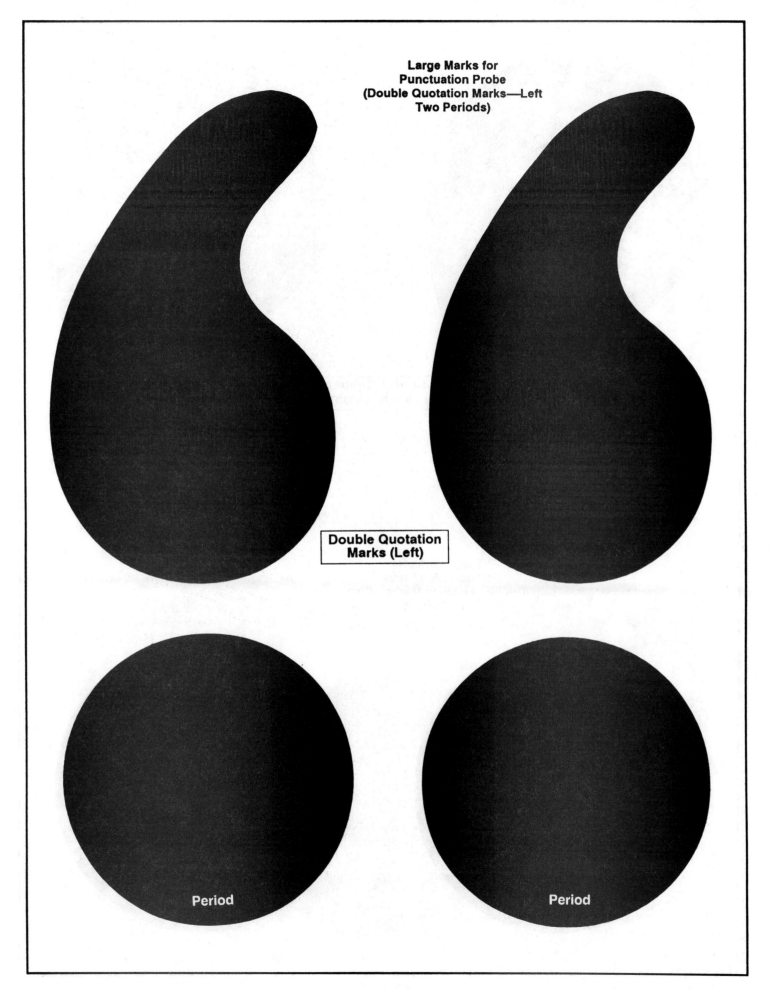

**Double Quotation
Marks (Left)**

Period

Period

GA1497

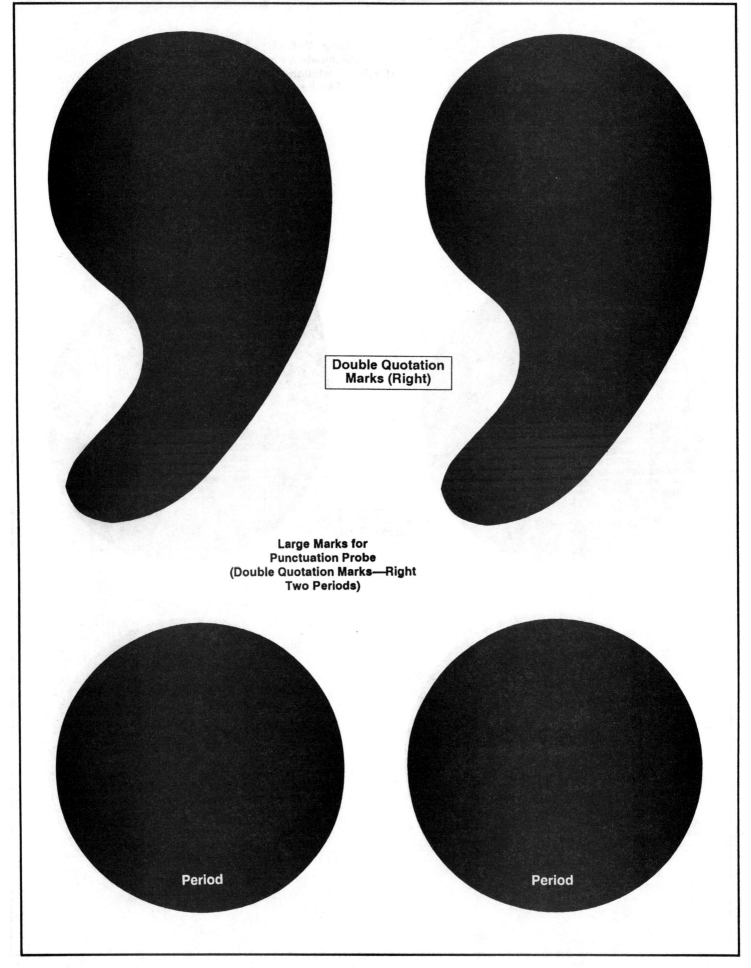

Double Quotation
Marks (Right)

**Large Marks for
Punctuation Probe
(Double Quotation Marks—Right
Two Periods)**

Period

Period

GA1497

**Large Marks for
Punctuation Probe
(Colon and Semicolon)**

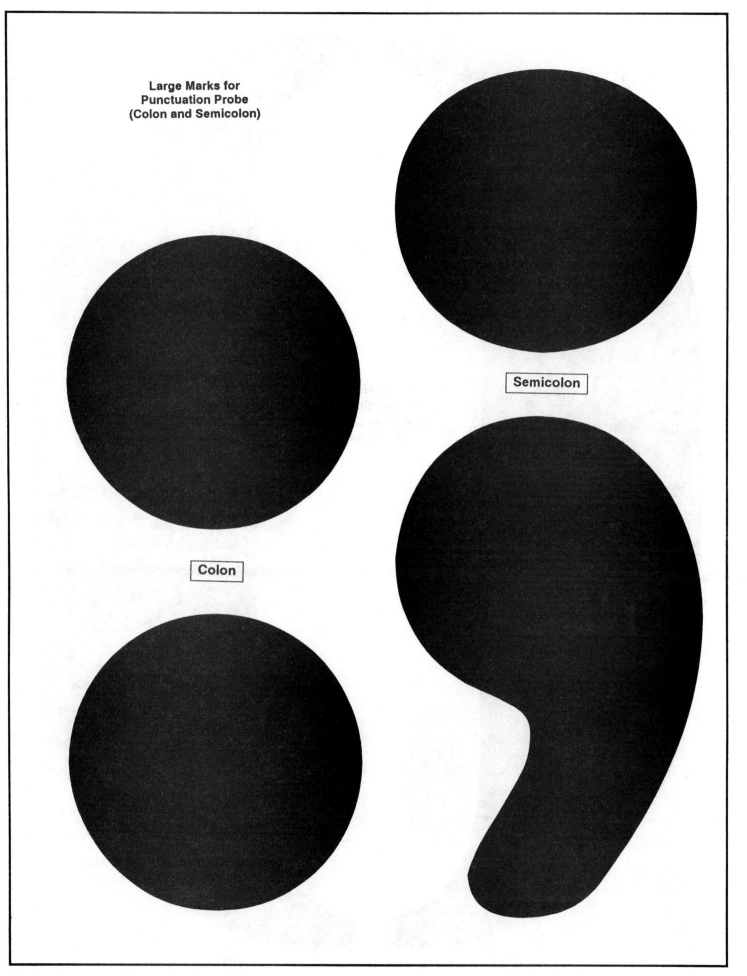

Semicolon

Colon

GA1497

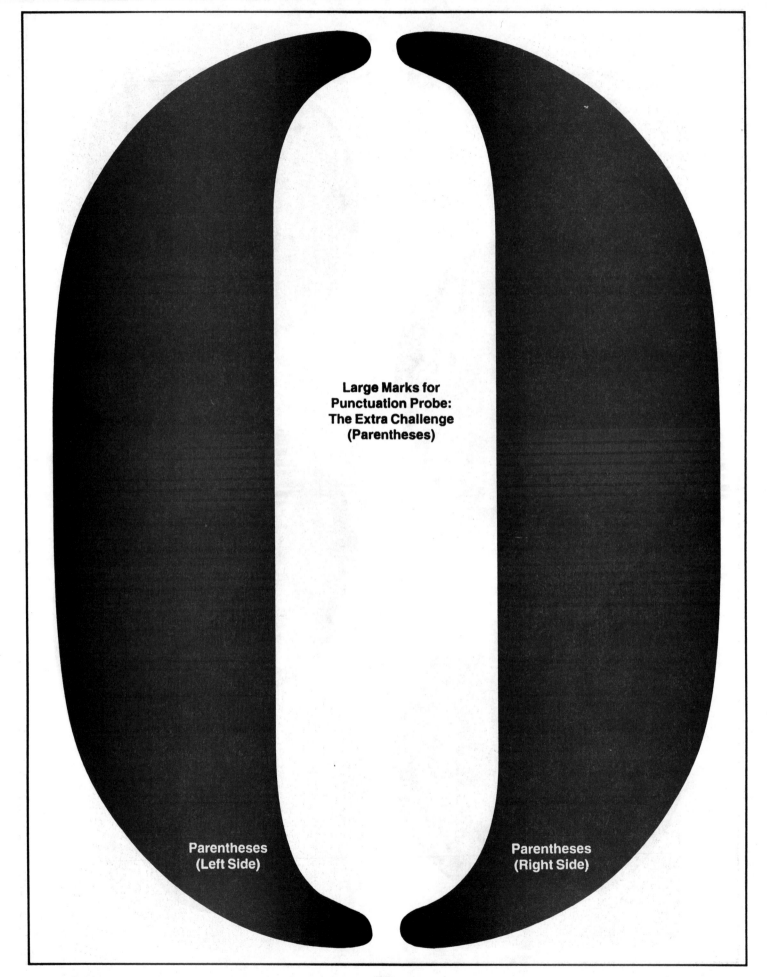

Large Marks for
Punctuation Probe:
The Extra Challenge
(Parentheses)

Parentheses
(Left Side)

Parentheses
(Right Side)

GA1497

**Large Marks for
Punctuation Probe:
The Unbelievable Challenge
(Hyphen, Dash, Ellipsis)**

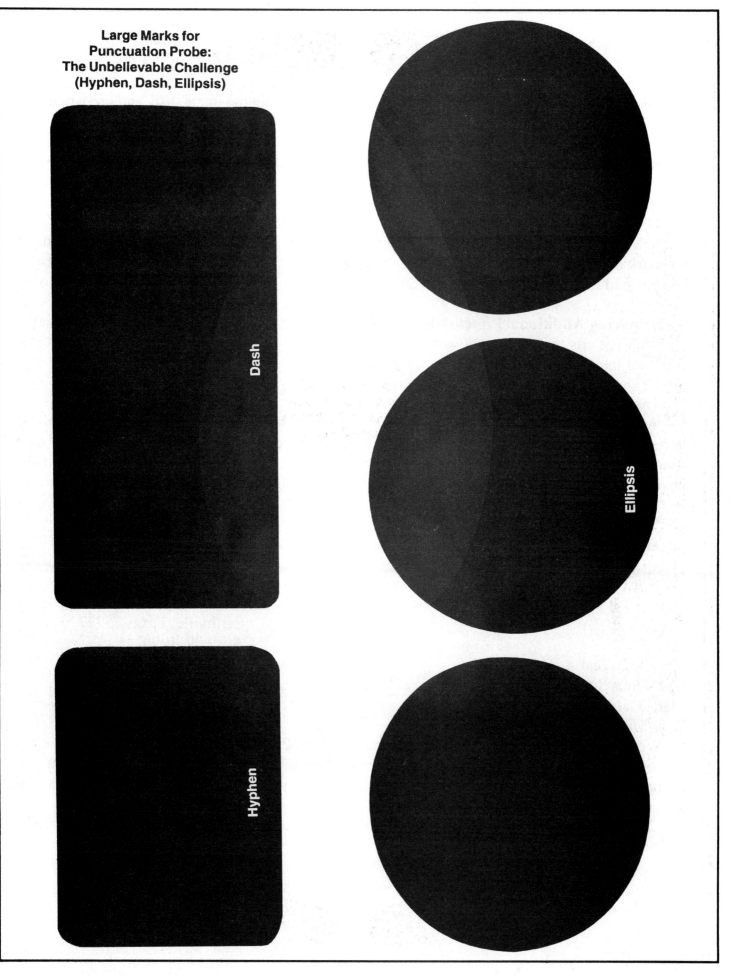

27

Punctuation Fill-In Fun

Please read pages 11-12 for complete information regarding the intent, use, and preparation of the Fill-In Fun Activities contained in this book.

Samples Provided for Punctuation Skills: The following Punctuation Fill-In Fun pages contain from twenty-five to thirty-three items for learners to complete. These pages may be used in early grades (with guided instruction) through the later grades as desired. Students should be encouraged to write their selected marks of punctuation very carefully in the blank spaces. For example, marks of punctuation such as the apostrophe could be easily confused with the comma if the mark is placed more toward the center than at the top or bottom. Periods and commas can also be confused if they are not written correctly.

Preparing Additional Punctuation Fill-In Fun Pages: Examine the punctuation material in the language arts textbooks and workbooks for your grade level. Consider turning some of these activities into Punctuation Fill-In Fun for your students.

Answers for Pages 29 and 30:

"My Teacher's Weird Trip": Last summer my teacher, Mrs. Earhead, took an unusual trip. She left on Monday, July 31, just after lunch. When she arrived at the airport, she learned she'd be flying on the top of a strange plane. High up in the sky she flew over Nevada and Utah. Next she flew over Colorado, Kansas, and Missouri. On Tuesday, August 8, at 4:30 p.m., she returned home.

"Were you scared?" we asked her.

"No, it was wonderful!" she shouted.

And that's the truth about Mrs. Earhead's strange trip.

"Far Out!":

P. O. Box 126
Earthville, Texas 75777
April 29, 1999

Mr. Ale E. Enn
000 Venus Street, Shuttle #2
Mars, Galaxy XZXY7

Dear Mr. Enn:

Wow! Thank you for your visit to our class on April 2, 1999, at 2:00 p.m. in the afternoon. I especially liked your story entitled "Not Enough Space." Becky, Joan, and Judy thought you sounded funny. Becky's friend Mark says it's difficult for you to speak English. Our cheerleaders' sponsor disagrees. Is it difficult?

Can you come back to our class next month on any Tuesday, Wednesday, or Friday? Please let us know.

Sincerely,

Earthling

Punctuation Fill-In Fun: (25) Name: _____

Student Instructions: In each blank space write a mark of punctuation—choosing only from one of the items in parentheses immediately below the blank. When only one choice is provided, you may either write that item in the blank or you may write nothing at all if no punctuation is needed in that spot. There is only one correct answer for each blank.

My Teacher's Weird Trip

Last summer my teacher, Mrs_ Earhead_ took an unusual trip_
(.)   (,)   (. ?)

She left on Monday_ July_ 31_ just after lunch. When she arrived at
(,)   (,)   (,)

the airport_ she learned she_d be flying on the top of a strange
(,)   (')

plane. High up in the sky she flew over Nevada_ and Utah. Next she
(,)

flew over Colorado_ Kansas_ and_ Missouri_   On Tuesday_
(,)   (,)   (,)   (, .)   (,)

August_ 8_ at 4_30 p_m., she returned home.
(,)   (,)   (, :)   (, .)

   "Were you scared_" we asked her_
          (. ?)   (. ?)

   "No_ it was wonderful_" she shouted_
     (. ,)   (. !)   (. !)

And that_s the truth about Mrs. Earhead_s strange trip.
    (')   (')

GA1497

Punctuation Fill-In Fun: (33) Name: _____

Student Instructions: In each blank space write a mark of punctuation—choosing only from one of the items in parentheses immediately below the blank. When only one choice is provided, you may either write that item in the blank or you may write nothing at all if no punctuation is needed in that spot. There is only one correct answer for each blank.

Far Out!

P. O_ Box 126
(. ,)

Earthville_ Texas_75777
(,)   (,)

April_ 29_1999
(,)   (,)

Mr_ Ale E_ Enn
(.)   (.)

000 Venus Street, Shuttle #2

Mars, Galaxy XZXY7

Dear Mr. Enn_
(, :)

    Wow_ Thank you for your visit_ to our class on
(. !)   (,)

April_ 2_ 1999_ at 2_00 p_m_ in the afternoon. I
(,)   (,)   (,)   (. :) (. ,)(. ,)

especially liked your story entitled _Not Enough
(, '')

Space._ Becky_ Joan_ and_ Judy_ thought you
('' !)   (,)   (,)   (,)   (,)

sounded funny. Becky_s_ friend Mark says_ it_s
(')(')   (,)   (')

difficult for you to speak English. Our cheerleader_s_
(')(')

sponsor disagrees. Is it difficult_
(. ?)

    Can you come back to our class next month on

any Tuesday_ Wednesday_ or Friday_ Please let
(,)   (,)   (. ?)

us know.

Sincerely_
(, :)

Earthling

Earthling

Punctuation Pop-Up Cards

Two sets of punctuation pop-up cards are provided later in this section. For preparation and general use of these cards, please read carefully pages 7-10.

Level A is for younger learners who have been introduced to the following four punctuation marks: the period, the question mark, the exclamation mark, and the comma. Level B is for older learners who have additionally studied the apostrophe, quotation marks, the colon, and the semicolon. Teachers do not need to delay the use of Level A punctuation pop-up cards until all four punctuation symbols have been studied. For example, the three end punctuation marks may be used before commas are introduced. This same idea applies to the cards provided in Level B.

The wording for the punctuation pop-up cards instructions may vary. Here is one possibility: "You have four cards on your desk. One of them has a period, one a question mark, one an exclamation mark, and one a comma. I will show you a sentence with one of those punctuation marks missing. Think about which one is needed. After you decide, please hold up that card without saying anything (and without looking around at the cards of others)." Show a sample sentence such as *Where are my shoes* (without a question mark). Allow adequate time for students to respond; then say, "That's right, this sentence needs a **question mark**. Now look at this next sentence."

Sentences for this activity may be written on the chalkboard, on sentence strips (for small-group instruction), or on transparency film to be used with the overhead projector. The sentences on the following page may be used as starters. An abundance of additional examples may be found in textbooks and workbooks.

31

GA1497

I am hungry

Why is your friend so sad

Get out fast before the bomb explodes

The event happened on March 3 1997.

The sad tired duck stopped quacking.

Mr Jones spoke softly.

Starters for Punctuation Pop-Up: (Level B—Those in Level A may also be used with B.)

Why arent we leaving?

Where are we going?" she asked.

Lunch will be ready at 1230 p.m.

Mom left however, Dad wanted to stay.

Johns car was stalled.

Then I screamed, "No! I won't go!

Answers: (A) period, question mark, exclamation mark, comma, comma, period;
(B) apostrophe, beginning quotation marks, colon, semicolon, apostrophe, ending quotation marks

Cards for Punctuation Pop-Up (Level A)

See page 10 for preparation instructions.

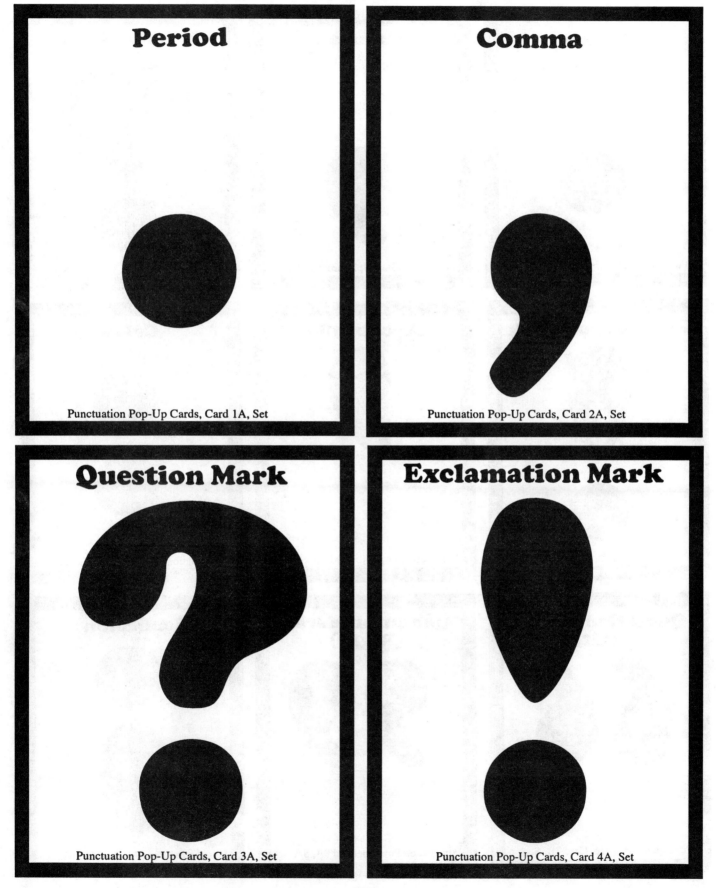

Period

Punctuation Pop-Up Cards, Card 1A, Set

Comma

Punctuation Pop-Up Cards, Card 2A, Set

Question Mark

Punctuation Pop-Up Cards, Card 3A, Set

Exclamation Mark

Punctuation Pop-Up Cards, Card 4A, Set

GA1497

Cards for Punctuation Pop-Up (Level B)
See page 10 for preparation instructions.

Period

Punctuation Pop-Up, Card 1B, Set

Comma

Punctuation Pop-Up, Card 2B, Set

Question Mark

Punctuation Pop-Up, Card 3B, Set

Exclamation Mark

Punctuation Pop-Up, Card 4B, Set

Apostrophe

Punctuation Pop-Up, Card 5B, Set

Colon

Punctuation Pop-Up, Card 6B, Set

Quotation Marks (Left)

Punctuation Pop-Up, Card 7B, Set

Quotation Marks (Right)

Punctuation Pop-Up, Card 8B, Set

Semicolon

Punctuation Pop-Up, Card 9B, Set

GA1497

Crazy Contractions

Teaching contractions is usually a difficult task. Young learners are often confused by the concept that the apostrophe in the contraction generally represents omitted letters. Only after the learner **sees** that the apostrophe has in fact replaced omitted letters is the concept generally understood. Crazy Contractions **shows** this idea.

Procedure: Use Crazy Contraction cards (pages 37 and 38) with an individual, a small group, or an entire class. Hold the flip card in view of all, with the apostrophe overlay forming the contraction. Ask learners to pronounce the word on the card. Remind them that the apostrophe takes the place of one or more omitted letters and/or spaces. Ask which letters and/or spaces the apostrophe replaces in the contraction you are holding. Then flip the apostrophe over the back to show the original words. In this manner the students can see the transformation in language that has occurred to create the contraction. To complete the process, turn the entire card over to show the word written as a contraction. (Do this in your own handwriting.) In addition to teaching punctuation, this activity helps in other language areas, such as spelling.

Preparation of Cards: Copy and cut the sample cards as indicated. They may first be photocopied onto stiff paper, then laminated for greater durability, if desired.

Preparation of Additional Cards: Numerous additional examples may be prepared. Index cards (5" x 8" [12.7 x 20.32 cm]) may be used. The list on page 36 provides material for these additional cards. Note that these listed words are non-noun contractions. Practically all nouns can be contracted; for example, the noun *John* turns into *John's* in contexts such as *John's going to be late again.* (Note that *John's* as a possessive *[John's car]* is a separate language concept.) Therefore, the exercise of Crazy Contractions might begin with pronoun/verb/adverb contractions.

GA1497

Groups of Non-Noun Contractions

(Note that most of the following contractions appear in more than one category.)

IS

he's (he is)
she's (she is)
it's (it is)
who's (who is)
where's (where is)
how's (how is)
that's (that is)
there's (there is)
here's (here is)
isn't (is not)
'tis (it is)

ARE

you're (you are)
we're (we are)
they're (they are)
aren't (are not)

HAVE

I've (I have)
you've (you have)
we've (we have)
they've (they have)
haven't (have not)

HAS

he's (hc has)
she's (she has)
it's (it has)
who's (who has)
where's (where has)
that's (that has)
there's (there has)
hasn't (has not)

HAD

I'd (I had)
you'd (you had)
he'd (he had)
she'd (she had)
we'd (we had)
they'd (they had)
who'd (who had)
hadn't (had not)

WILL

I'll (I will)
you'll (you will)
he'll (he will)
she'll (she will)
it'll (it will)
we'll (we will)
they'll (they will)
who'll (who will)
won't (will not)

WOULD

I'd (I would)
you'd (you would)
he'd (he would)
she'd (she would)
we'd (we would)
they'd (they would)
who'd (who would)
wouldn't (would not)

NOT

isn't (is not)
aren't (are not)
haven't (have not)
hasn't (has not)
hadn't (had not)
won't (will not)
wouldn't (would not)
couldn't (could not)
shouldn't (should not)
can't (can not)
wasn't (was not)
weren't (were not)
doesn't (does not)
don't (do not)
didn't (did not)
mustn't (must not)

I

I've (I have)
I'd (I had or I would)
I'll (I will or I shall)
I'm (I am)

WE

we're (we are)
we've (we have)
we'd (we had or we would)
we'll (we will or we shall)

YOU

you're (you are)
you've (you have)
you'd (you had or you would)
you'll (you will)

HE

he's (he is or he has)
he'd (he had or he would)
he'll (he will)

SHE

she's (she is or she has)
she'd (she had or she would)
she'll (she will)

IT

it's (it is or it has)
it'll (it will)
'tis (it is)
'twas (it was)

THEY

they're (they are)
they've (they have)
they'd (they had or they would)
they'll (they will)

WHO

who's (who is or who has)
who'd (who had or who would)
who'll (who will)

Miscellaneous

let's (let us)
o'clock (of the clock)

GA1497

Crazy Contraction Cards

Use this card
as the apostrophe
flap for *I am (I'm)*.

Use this card
as the apostrophe
flap for *we will (we'll)*.

Use this card
as the apostrophe
flap for *they are (they're)*.

I am

we will

they are

GA1497

More Crazy Contraction Cards

Use this card as the apostrophe flap for *it is (it's).*

Use this card as the apostrophe flap for *you have (you've).*

Use this card as the apostrophe flap for *of the clock (o'clock).*

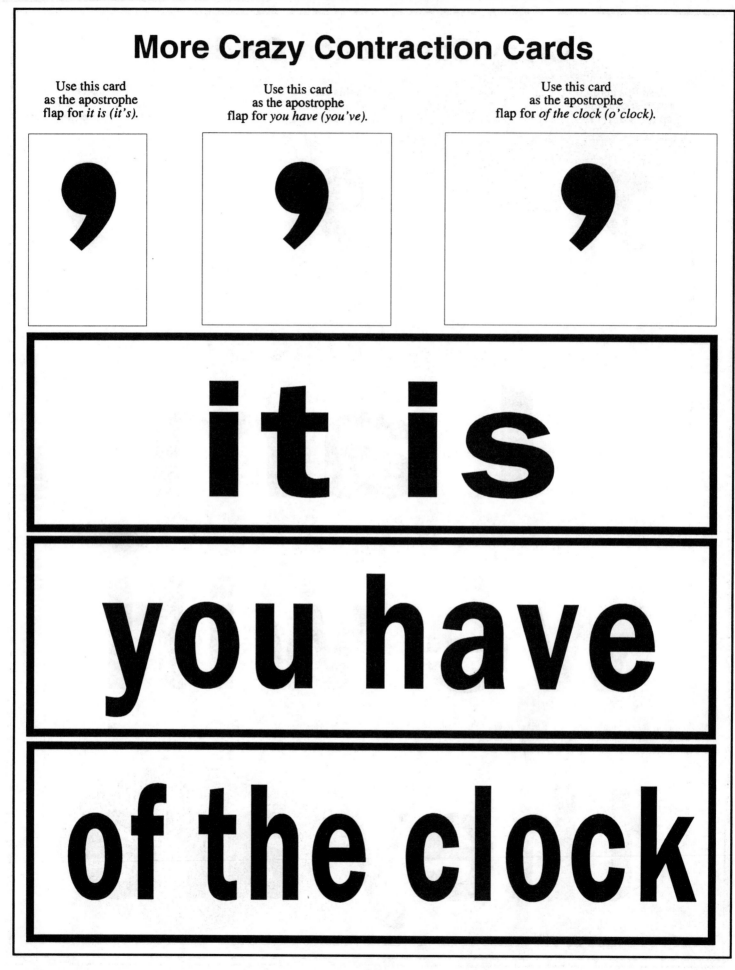

it is

you have

of the clock

GA1497

Activities
for
Teaching
CAPITALIZATION

GA1497

Capitalization—just like punctuation—is a skill used by writers only. Again, the activities used to teach this part of language mechanics must be _seen_ by the learners in order for these mechanical skills to be mastered. Have fun with these suggestions.

Capitalization Pop-Up Cards

Pop-up cards containing the lowercase and uppercase letters are provided for capitalization experiences. For preparation and general use of these cards, please read carefully pages 7-10. Items for this activity may be written on the chalkboard, on sentence strips, or on transparency film to be used with the overhead projector.

The actual activities for the capitalization pop-up cards may vary. The standard method (as suggested for the other pop-up activities in this book) may be used. Due to the number of cards with the capitalization activities, the following variations are offered for the capitalization sets:

Select only a few letters of the alphabet to give to each student. Proceed with the regular activity. The instructional wording for such an activity may vary. Here is one possibility: "Each one of you has a capital *B* and a lowercase *b* on your desk. Who can tell us the difference in the two? (Allow time for responses.) I am going to show you (or say) a word that starts with the letter *b*. This word is written with all capital letters so we do not know if the first letter should really be a capital. Look at the word and hold up the capital *B* if you think it would be needed for this word, or hold up the lowercase *b* if you think that would be correct. Let's start with the word *BOY*. Hold up your cards. (Allow time.) That's right, it is the lowercase *b*. Now look at (or listen to) the word *BETTY*. Would it need a capital *B* or a lowercase *b* if we used it in the middle of a sentence? (Allow time.) That's right . . ." Continue with words appropriate for the learners' levels of development.

GA1497

Place both the uppercase and lowercase sets of letters on a large table (or on the floor) in the classroom. Have the students gather around the table for a variation of the standard activity. The instructional wording for such an activity may vary. Here is one possibility: "There are fifty-two letters on this table. Twenty-six are lowercase letters and twenty-six are uppercase letters. Who can tell us the difference in the two? (Allow time for responses.) I am going to show you (or say) a word that is written with all capital letters so we do not know if the first letter should really be a capital. Find the letter on this table that would be needed if we were to write this word in the middle of a sentence. Look at that letter. In a few seconds I will ask one of you to point to that letter. The first word is . . ."

Write a sentence that contains some words needing capital letters. Write each word without an initial letter, and write each word on a separate card. Place these prepared cards on a chalk tray (or on the floor). Ask students to find the letters that should begin each word and place them in the appropriate positions.

Have students turn to a page in their textbooks or workbooks that is intended to teach capitalization skills. Instead of having them copy the sentences using appropriate capitalization or having them complete workbook pages, identify a sentence for all class members to turn to. Then ask, "What is the first capital letter that is needed in this sentence? See who can find this letter and hold it up."

Distribute the fifty-two cards (as equally as possibly) among the students. Point to the initial letter of a word written on a card or say a word. Have the student who has the appropriate uppercase or lowercase letter stand up (or "pop up") and hold up the card.

Tape the fifty-two letters around the wall in the classroom (or wall of the cafeteria or gymnasium). Give the word in question and ask the students to see who can first touch the appropriate letter. Be aware, however, that students can become quite rowdy with this choice.

(A special note to those clever teachers who will see these alphabet cards and decide to use them for spelling activities. That is a good idea, but be aware of the fact that you will need to make several sets in order to have enough letters to spell words with repeated letters. There are many additional uses for these cards, such as alphabetization experiences. You are limited only by your own imagination.)

Some Starters for Capitalization Pop-Ups:

(J or j) ___ anuary

(F or f) ___ ebruary

(M or m) ___ arch

(A or a) ___ pril

(M or m) ___ ay

(J or j) ___ une

(J or j) ___ uly

(A or a) ___ ugust

(S or s) ___ eptember

(O or o) ___ ctober

(N or n) ___ ovember

(D or d) ___ ecember

(S or s) ___ unday

(M or m) ___ onday

(T or t) ___ uesday

(W or w) ___ ednesday

(T or t) ___ hursday

(F or f) ___ riday

(S or s) ___ aturday

Some A or a words:

(A or a) ___ laska

(A or a) ___ nn

(A or a) ___ llen

(A or a) ___ nt

(A or a) ___ ctor

GA1497

Some B or b words:

(B or b) ___ ird

(B or b) ___ urt

(B or b) ___ oy

(B or b) ___ at

(B or b) ___ uilding

(B or b) ___ arbara

Some D or d words:

(D or d) ___ og

(D or d) ___ ove Street

(D or d) ___ uck

(D or d) ___ ennis

(D or d) ___ elaware

(D or d) ___ esk

Some C or c words:

(C or c) ___ at

(C or c) ___ alifornia

(C or c) ___ ar

(C or c) ___ hina

(C or c) ___ hicago

(C or c) ___ andy

Some N or n words:

(N or n) ___ ancy

(N or n) ___ ew York

(N or n) ___ est

(N or n) ___ ame

(N or n) ___ ebraska

(N or n) ___ eighbor

Continue with other letters as desired.

GA1497

Cards for Capitalization Pop-Up: Uppercase Letters

See page 10 for preparation instructions.

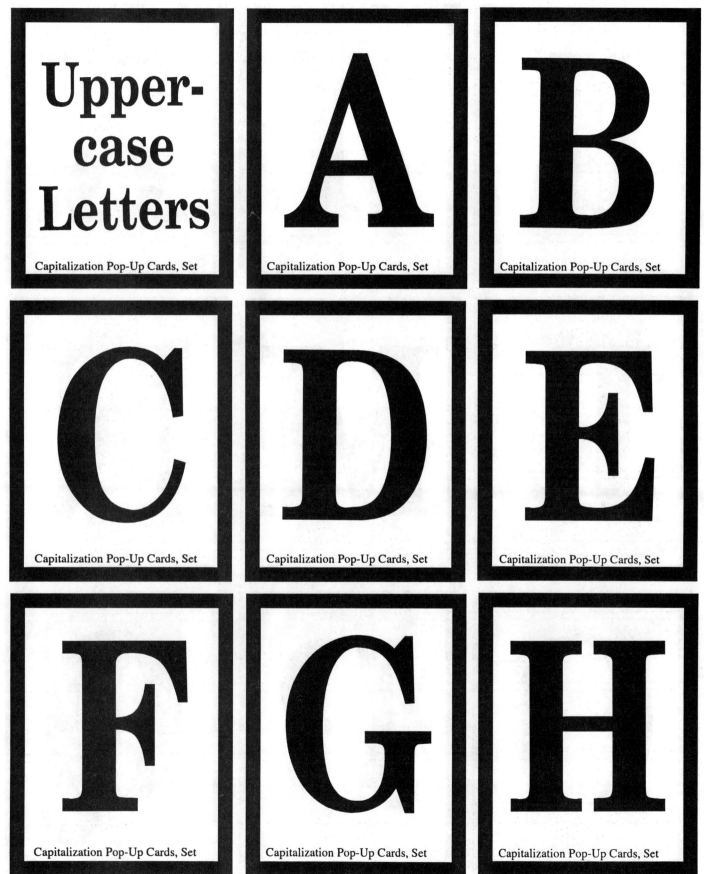

Upper-case Letters

Capitalization Pop-Up Cards, Set

A

Capitalization Pop-Up Cards, Set

B

Capitalization Pop-Up Cards, Set

C

Capitalization Pop-Up Cards, Set

D

Capitalization Pop-Up Cards, Set

E

Capitalization Pop-Up Cards, Set

F

Capitalization Pop-Up Cards, Set

G

Capitalization Pop-Up Cards, Set

H

Capitalization Pop-Up Cards, Set

GA1497

Cards for Capitalization Pop-Up: Uppercase Letters (Continued)

See page 10 for preparation instructions.

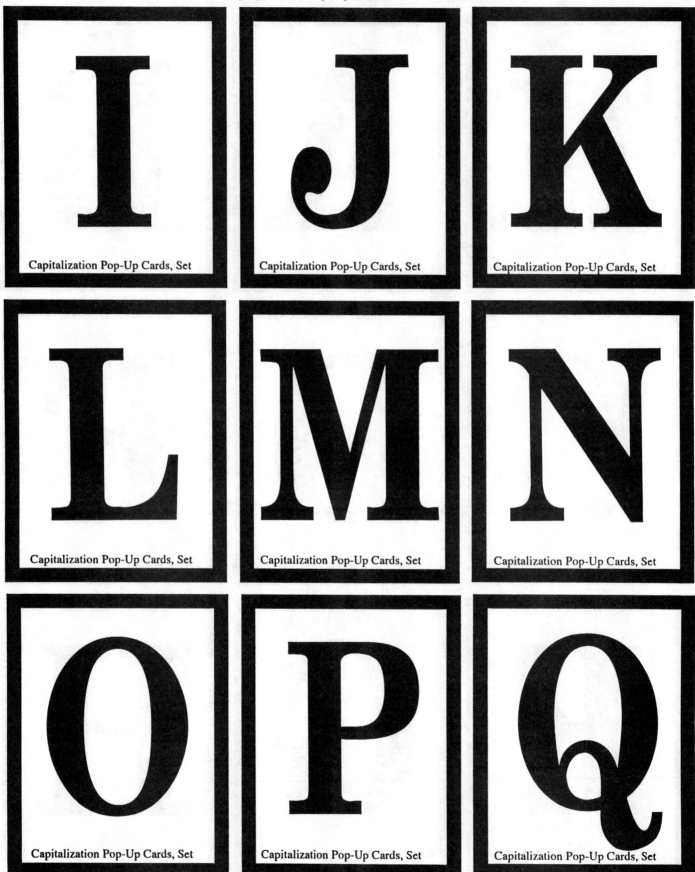

Capitalization Pop-Up Cards, Set

Capitalization Pop-Up Cards, Set

Capitalization Pop-Up Cards, Set

Capitalization Pop-Up Cards, Set

Capitalization Pop-Up Cards, Set

Capitalization Pop-Up Cards, Set

Capitalization Pop-Up Cards, Set

Capitalization Pop-Up Cards, Set

Capitalization Pop-Up Cards, Set

GA1497

Cards for Capitalization Pop-Up: Uppercase Letters (Continued)

See page 10 for preparation instructions.

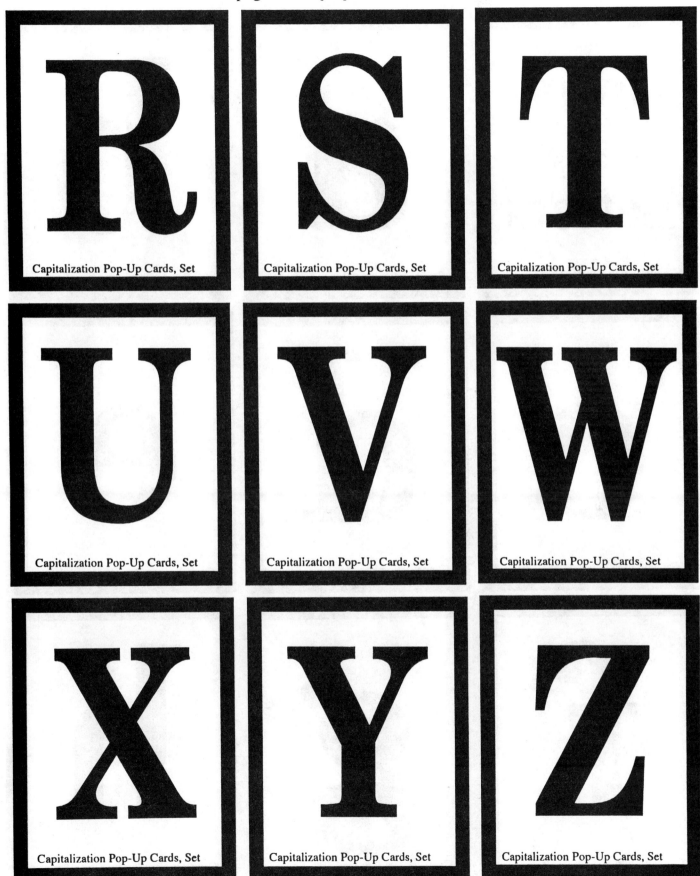

Capitalization Pop-Up Cards, Set

Capitalization Pop-Up Cards, Set

Capitalization Pop-Up Cards, Set

Capitalization Pop-Up Cards, Set

Capitalization Pop-Up Cards, Set

Capitalization Pop-Up Cards, Set

Capitalization Pop-Up Cards, Set

Capitalization Pop-Up Cards, Set

Capitalization Pop-Up Cards, Set

Cards for Capitalization Pop-Up: Lowercase Letters
See page 10 for preparation instructions.

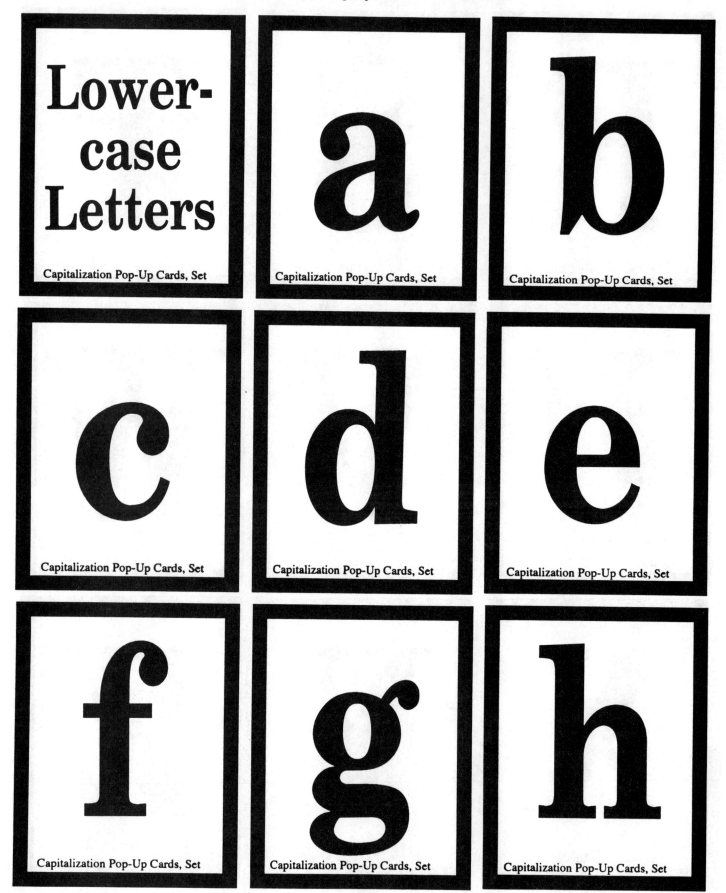

Lower-case Letters

Capitalization Pop-Up Cards, Set

a

Capitalization Pop-Up Cards, Set

b

Capitalization Pop-Up Cards, Set

c

Capitalization Pop-Up Cards, Set

d

Capitalization Pop-Up Cards, Set

e

Capitalization Pop-Up Cards, Set

f

Capitalization Pop-Up Cards, Set

g

Capitalization Pop-Up Cards, Set

h

Capitalization Pop-Up Cards, Set

GA1497

See page 10 for preparation instructions.

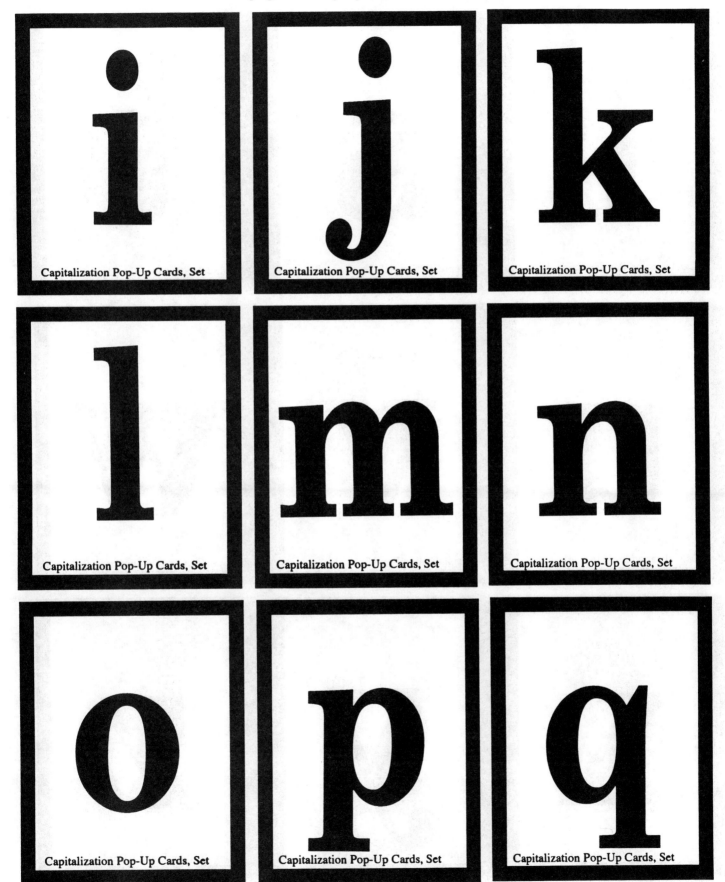

i

Capitalization Pop-Up Cards, Set

j

Capitalization Pop-Up Cards, Set

k

Capitalization Pop-Up Cards, Set

l

Capitalization Pop-Up Cards, Set

m

Capitalization Pop-Up Cards, Set

n

Capitalization Pop-Up Cards, Set

o

Capitalization Pop-Up Cards, Set

p

Capitalization Pop-Up Cards, Set

q

Capitalization Pop-Up Cards, Set

GA1497

Cards for Capitalization Pop-Up: Lowercase Letters (Continued)

See page 10 for preparation instructions.

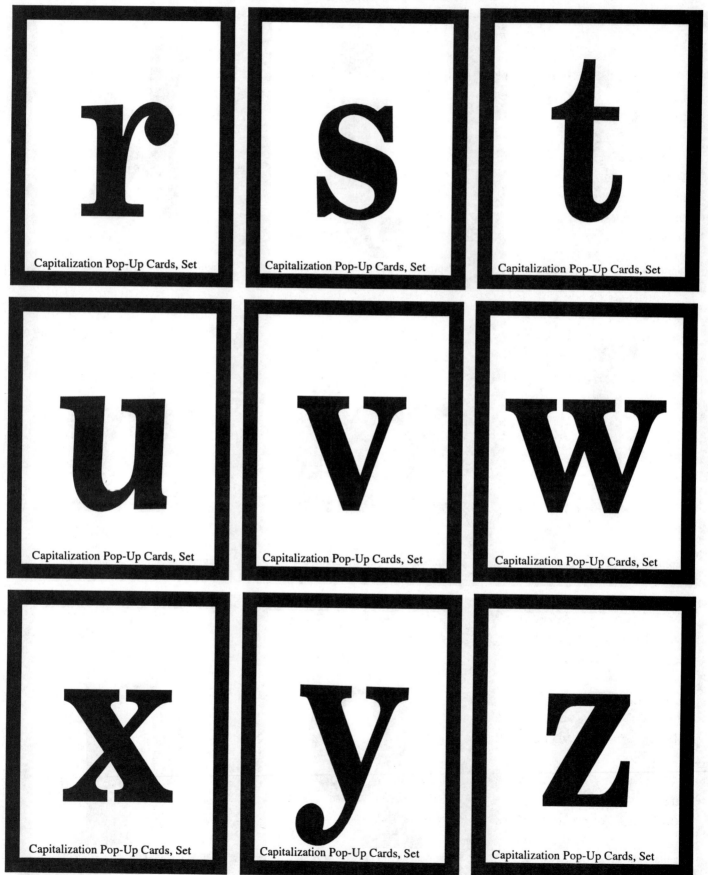

r

Capitalization Pop-Up Cards, Set

s

Capitalization Pop-Up Cards, Set

t

Capitalization Pop-Up Cards, Set

u

Capitalization Pop-Up Cards, Set

v

Capitalization Pop-Up Cards, Set

w

Capitalization Pop-Up Cards, Set

x

Capitalization Pop-Up Cards, Set

y

Capitalization Pop-Up Cards, Set

z

Capitalization Pop-Up Cards, Set

GA1497

Capitalization Fill-In Fun

Please read pages 11-12 for complete information regarding the intent, use, and preparation of the Fill-In Fun Activities contained in this book.

The following Capitalization Fill-In Fun pages contain from ten to thirty-three items for learners to complete. These pages may be used in early grades (with guided instruction) through the later grades as desired.

A Special Instructional Note: As learners complete these pages, encourage them to be very careful to make their capital letters much larger than their lowercase letters. With letters such as *c* or *s*, some very astute writers seem to go midway between the two sizes and later argue that the correct answer was the one they intended. Perhaps they are to be admired for their cleverness, but this should be avoided when at all possible. Letters such as *g*, *i*, or *q* are not as similar in appearance in their uppercase and lowercase forms.

Samples Provided for Capitalization Skills: There are five samples of Fill-In Fun activities for capitalization on pages 54-58. The first is a ten-item story with the uppercase and lowercase *B*. The second is on the same level, but it involves the uppercase and lowercase *D*. The third is slightly more advanced with thirty blanks of various letters. The remaining two are also on a higher grade level, each having thirty-three blanks. The last one includes the capitalization necessary for most friendly letters.

Preparing Additional Capitalization Fill-In Fun Pages: Examine the capitalization material in the language arts textbooks and workbooks for your grade level. Consider turning some of these activities into Capitalization Fill-In Fun for your students.

Answers for Pages 54-58:
"Bully, the Boa Constrictor": boy, Billy, Black, bear, Betty, Bunny, beasts, Boa, Bully, big.

"The Jailhouse Dog": Dade, Day, dog, Do, Danny, Dog, dug, Dog's, Donald, December.

"National Egghead Day": Beak, Claw, School, holiday, National, Egghead, Day, Wednesday, May, Eggbert, president, Henrietta, Chickee, president, school, Mrs., principal, Polly, Pullet, secretary, newspaper, The, Rooster, Roster, holiday, weeks, day, event, Drumstick, Circle.

"Tom's Cruise": friend, cruise, Joy, Rider, Monday, July, Wednesday, August, ship, Cuba, Rico, Jamaica, French, restaurant, Spanish, fort, Tom, songs, countries, Star, Spangled, Banner, cabin, African, storyteller, Uncle, Remus, tales, captain, Fourth, July, Americans, I.

"A Letter to Elvis": Main, Street, Ohio, November, Dear, mom, newspaper, City, Times, and, Saturday, Memphis, Tennessee, aunt, Sweet, month, Burger, King, Graceland, year, summer, months, Grandmother, Me, Tender, I, grandmother, great, aunt, Be, Cruel, Yours, truly.

Student Instructions: Write a capital *B* or a lowercase *b* in each of the blank spaces.

Bully, the Boa Constrictor

One day a little __oy named __illy felt brave. He walked to __lack Forest. First he saw a __ear. Next he saw __etty __unny. Then he saw a boa constrictor. The forest __easts all called him Bully __oa. Billy walked up to __ully and loudly asked him for a __ig hug. Uh . . . Oh . . . What do you think happened to Billy?

GA1497

Student Instructions: Write a capital *D* or a lowercase *d* in each of the blank spaces.

The Jailhouse Dog

Danny Dog was in deep trouble. He was in the __ade County Jail on Labor __ay. Danny denied doing any bad deed. His __og friends asked the judge, "__o you know why __anny __og is in jail?"

The judge answered, "Yes, he __ug up Donald __og's bones. __onald will let him out in __ecember."

GA1497

Capitalization Fill-In Fun: (30) Name: _____

Student Instructions: In each blank space write one of the letters from the choices in parentheses immediately below the blank.

National Egghead Day

Our school, __eak and __law Poultry __chool, has declared a new
      (B b)   (C c)   (S s)

__oliday. It is __ational __gghead __ay, to be celebrated on
(H h)   (N n)   (E e)   (D d)

__ednesday, __ay 12. __ggbert Einstein, the class __resident, wrote
(W w)   (M m)   (E e)   (P p)

the rules for this day; __enrietta __hickee, the vice-__resident,
               (H h)   (C c)   (P p)

planned the __chool parade; __rs. Shell, our school __rincipal, sent
       (S s)   (M m)   (P p)

announcements home to all parents; and __olly __ullet, the school
                          (P p) (P p)

__ecretary, established the
(S s)

pecking order for the event.

The school __ewspaper, __he
      (N n)   (T t)

__ooster __oster, advertised
(R r)   (R r)

the __oliday for several __eeks in
   (H h)   (W w)

advance. Everyone was quite

excited.

On the __ay of the big __vent
     (D d)   (E e)

everyone noticed something

strange. Near the corner of

__rumstick Boulevard and Corn
(D d)

__ircle, an unusual egg was about
(C c)

to hatch. Folks gathered around

to watch. What, eggsactly, do you

think happened next?

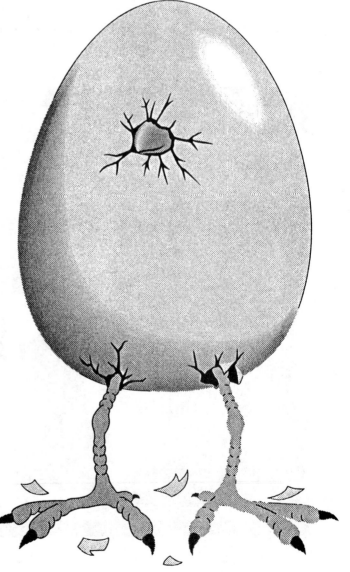

Student Instructions: In each blank space write one of the letters from the choices in parentheses immediately below the blank.

Tom's Cruise

My __riend Tom has just
(F f)

returned from a __ruise on the __oy
(C c)   (J j)

__ider. He left on __onday, __uly 2,
(R r)   (M m)   (J j)

and returned on __ednesday,
(W w)

__ugust 1. The __hip stopped at
(A a)   (S s)

__uba, Haiti, Puerto __ico, and
(C c)   (R r)

__amaica. Tom ate at a __rench
(J j)   (F f)

__estaurant, and he toured a
(R r)

__panish __ort.
(S s)   (F f)

   Then __om listened to __ongs
        (T t)   (S s)

from the other __ountries, and he
(C c)

sang "The __tar-__pangled
(S s) (S s)

__anner" for those in his __abin.
(B b)   (C c)

An __frican __toryteller told some
(A a)   (S s)

__ncle __emus __ales. The ship's
(U u)   (R r)   (T t)

__aptain, Leonel Garcia, then
(C c)

announced a special __ourth of
(F f)

__uly party for the __mericans on
(J j)   (A a)

board.

   Never will __ forget hearing
              (I i)

the stories about Tom's cruise.

Have you heard any?

GA1497

Student Instructions: In each blank space write one of the letters from the choices in parentheses immediately below the blank.

A Letter to Elvis

336 __ain __treet
(M m) (S s)

Apartment 17

Mytown, __hio 45840
(O o)

__ovember 4, 1999
(N n)

__ear Elvis,
(D d)

    It's time to settle the matter once and for all about whether you

are alive. My __om kept a 1977 __ewspaper, The Plain __ity __imes
(M m)   (N n)   (C c) (T t)

__nd News, that announced your death. The article also said that
(A a)

you were buried the following __aturday in __emphis, __ennessee.
(S s)   (M m)   (T t)

    However, my great __unt, Bessie __weet, swears she saw you last
(A a)   (S s)

__onth at the __urger __ing. She always visits __raceland mansion
(M m)   (B b)   (K k)   (G g)

each __ear during one of the __ummer __onths. __randmother says
(Y y)   (S s)   (M m)   (G g)

you sing "Love __e __ender" to her sometimes. Are they crazy?
(M m) (T t)

    If you are alive, please write and let me know. I promise __ won't
(I i)

tell anyone, not even my __randmother or __reat-__unt.
(G g)   (G g) (A a)

    By the way, I sing "Don't __e __ruel" to my mom when she tries to
(B b) (C c)

punish me. It seems to bring a smile to her lips.

__ours __ruly,
(Y y)   (T t)

ann

Ann Add Mirer

GA1497

Activities
for
Teaching
GRAMMAR

59

Grammar is a lifetime task! No one ever becomes flawless in its use. Those who study it, however, gradually become more knowledgeable of its intricacies and idiosyncrasies. These fun activities will assist young learners in this gradual process.

Sentence Wheels

A very motivating format for students learning the mechanical aspects of grammar is the "wheel." Each wheel contains identified grammatical concepts in a category that has been studied by the class. This format takes the place of traditional work sheets and it can create hours of competitive (or noncompetitive) fun in an area of study frequently dreaded by learners.

Classroom Procedures: Prepare the Sentence Wheels according to the instructions on the following page. The basic idea is for students to twirl each wheel, land on one of the items on each wheel, then write only *one* sentence that contains *all* of the twirled items. (This is tougher than you think. Try it!) When groups are used, one person from each group can write the group-prepared sentence on the chalkboard after all sentences have been thought through. Scoring can occur by giving all groups ten points at first, then deducting one point for each sentence element that doesn't fit what was twirled. No individual embarrassment is caused with this procedure because all students view all sentences from their seats. (Each group member can blame the others for any errors.) Another advantage of group work is the peer tutoring that invariably occurs in the process of writing a sentence. For example, if the group must write a sentence that contains a direct object, someone in the group can re-explain this concept to anyone who has forgotten it. After much group writing has occurred, then the boards may be twirled for sentence writing by individuals.

Selecting Boards: Examine the boards provided on pages 63-73. Select those with concepts your students have already studied or those they will be learning soon. Individual classrooms will need to make modifications according to many language and student factors. For this reason, several blank boards are provided on pages 74-78 for quick preparation of additional (or modified) items.

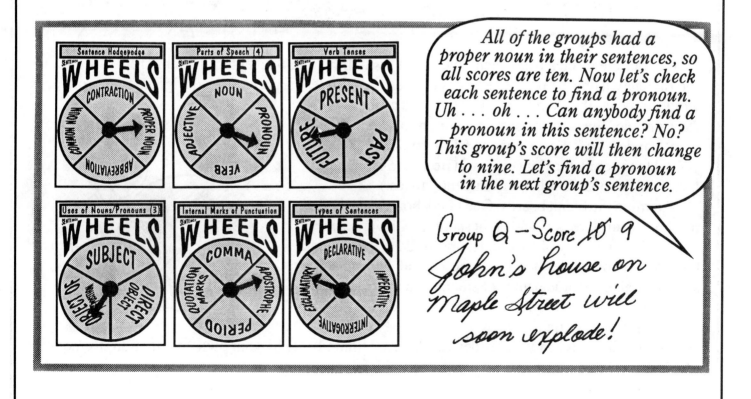

GA1497

Preparation of Sentence Wheels: There are several ways to prepare these wheels. In all cases the pages should be photocopied onto stiff paper—or copied onto regular paper and later mounted onto heavier paper—for durability and permanence. You might also want to protect the boards with laminating film or clear, self-adhesive paper. The following are some considerations in the preparation of these wheels:

Attach spinners to the photocopied boards. Be sure to attach loosely so the spinner is not too tight to spin freely around the board several times. The boards will likely need to lie flat rather than being held in the air in order for the spinners not to be affected by gravity and always land on the same item.

Prepare boards without spinners. Place them on the floor and have a penny toss to determine the items chosen. You will need a penny (or a substitute) for each board you have.

The pennies that Jake, Mike, and Theresa tossed onto our Sentence Wheels landed on adjective, contraction, and past tense. In your group write only one sentence that has an adjective, a contraction, and a verb in the past tense. You must have all three in one sentence. We will write each sentence on the chalkboard when all groups are ready.

Cut out the circles from each board. Cut a small hole in the center of each circle. This allows for finger twirling or nose twirling. For these two styles, a previously designated area of focus would indicate the item to be selected. For a finger twirl, for example, the item closest to the thumb would be the item "landed on." For a nose twirl, it could be the item closest to the chin, the right eye, etc. (Be aware of sanitation factors if the boards touch the students' faces.)

Examine the blank boards. One blank board is provided for three, four, five, six, and eight sections. Clever teachers will think of a variety of different items to add to these blank boards. For example, adding some capital letters, some story characters, some names of students in the classroom, and so on, can cause quite an interesting addition to the sentences being written.

Modify the above in any way desired. You are limited only by your own imagination! Remember that learning grammar *can* be fun and exciting!

SENTENCE WHEELS

GA1497

Sentence Hodgepodge

SENTENCE WHEELS

SENTENCE WHEELS

GA1497

SENTENCE WHEELS

COMMA

APOSTROPHE

PERIOD

QUOTATION MARKS

SENTENCE WHEELS

GA1497

SENTENCE WHEELS

DECLARATIVE

IMPERATIVE

INTERROGATIVE

EXCLAMATORY

GA1497

Types of Verbs

SENTENCE **WHEELS**

REGULAR

INTRANSITIVE

IRREGULAR

TRANSITIVE

SENTENCE WHEELS

GA1497

Sentences Forms

SENTENCE WHEELS

SIMPLE

COMPOUND

COMPLEX

COMPOUND-COMPLEX

SENTENCE WHEELS

GA1497

Parts of Speech (8)

SENTENCE WHEELS

GA1497

SENTENCE WHEELS

GA1497

SENTENCE **WHEELS**

76

GA1497

78

Grammar Fill-In Fun

Please read pages 11-12 for complete information regarding the intent, use, and preparation of the Fill-In Fun Activities contained in this book.

Samples Provided for Grammar Skills: Three Grammar Fill-In Fun pages containing from ten to twenty items are provided for learners to complete. These pages may be used as soon as learners have studied the concepts contained in the requested blanks. "The Day Our Car Quit" involves selected parts of speech, complete subjects and predicates, proper nouns, direct objects, and objects of prepositions. "A New Kind of Pizza" adds common nouns, plural nouns, and subject complements to these skills. "The Substitute Teacher" adds intransitive verbs, action verbs, and predicate adjectives to these skills. Substitutions may be provided for students who have not studied one or more of the skills requested. For example, in a class that has not yet discussed predicate adjectives, the word *predicate* may be removed and the word *adjective* left for the requested item.

Preparing Additional Grammar Fill-In Fun Pages: Examine the grammar material in the language arts textbooks and workbooks for your grade level. Consider turning some of these activities into Grammar Fill-In Fun pages for your students. As soon as simple subjects and simple predicates have been introduced, for example, Grammar Fill-In Fun pages may be created. Just these two concepts could be the basis for dozens of additional fun activities. When complete subjects and complete predicates have been introduced, more may be added. As each new grammar skill is studied, consider adding more pages of these activities.

Scoring and Checking Pages 80-82: Scoring these Fill-In Fun pages will be slightly different from the other Fill-In Fun pages provided in this book. All of the other skill areas have one and only one correct answer for each blank space. There is little or no creativity allowed on the part of the learners. With this section, however, a variety of different answers will be correct. In fact, this skill area is a complementary skill for creative writing. When asking students to write a complete subject, for example, you will need to accept anything that grammatically fits the blank area.

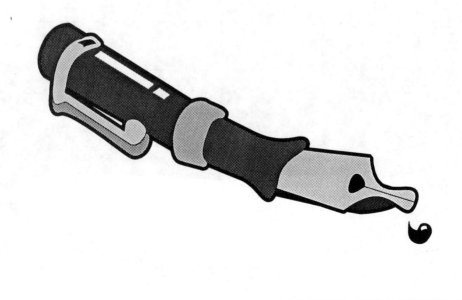

GA1497

Student Instructions: In each of the blank spaces write your choice of one or more words fitting the descriptions in parentheses.

The Day Our Car Quit

This morning when our family got into our old car, it just wouldn't

start. _____ *said it was too*
(complete subject)

_____ *to run any more. We looked across the*
(adjective)

_____ *and saw an old army tank.*
(noun)

_____ *got in it and started the engine. Then we all*
(proper noun)

piled in and rode to _____. *We waved at*
(object of preposition)

_____, *and then we* _____.
(proper noun)   (complete predicate)

Suddenly we heard a _____ *behind us.*
(direct object)

_____ *drove faster, but soon we were*
(proper noun)

_____.
(complete predicate)

That is a day I will never forget!

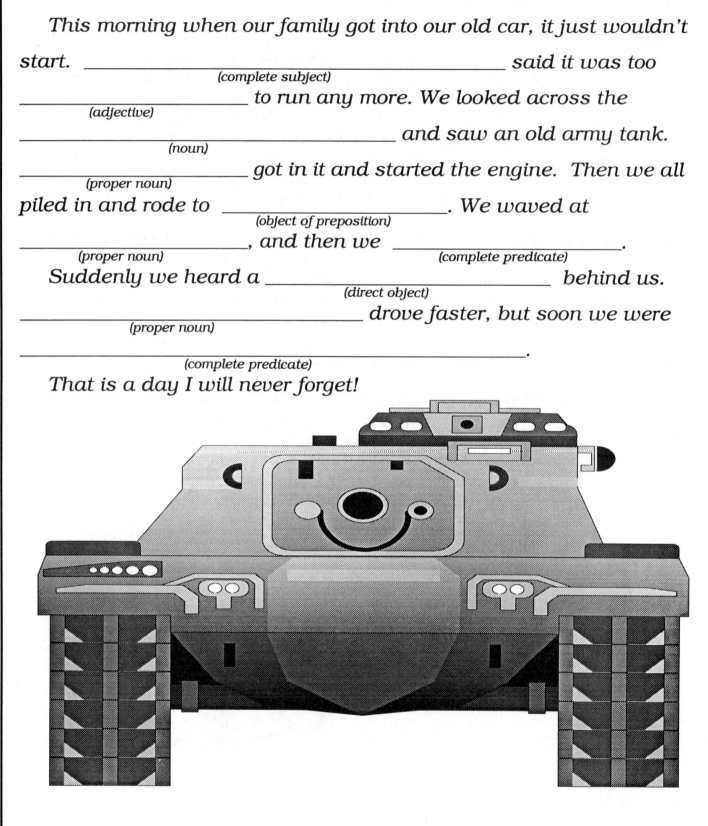

GA1497

Student Instructions: In each of the blank spaces write your choice of one or more words fitting the descriptions in parentheses.

A New Kind of Pizza

One day my friend wanted to make a new kind of pizza. She

made the crust, and then she began piling on toppings. I couldn't

believe it when I saw her put _____ on the crust.
(direct object)

The _____ she put on next looked like
(common noun)

_____. I almost _____ when I
(noun)   (verb)

watched her add _____.
(plural noun)

I was feeling rather _____ as I watched the last
(adjective)

item go on. It was _____.
(subject complement)

Next she decided to invite some friends to eat the pizza with us. I

wanted her to invite _____. Instead, she called
(proper noun)

_____. I must say that after I ate the pizza, it tasted
(any noun)

really _____.
(adjective)

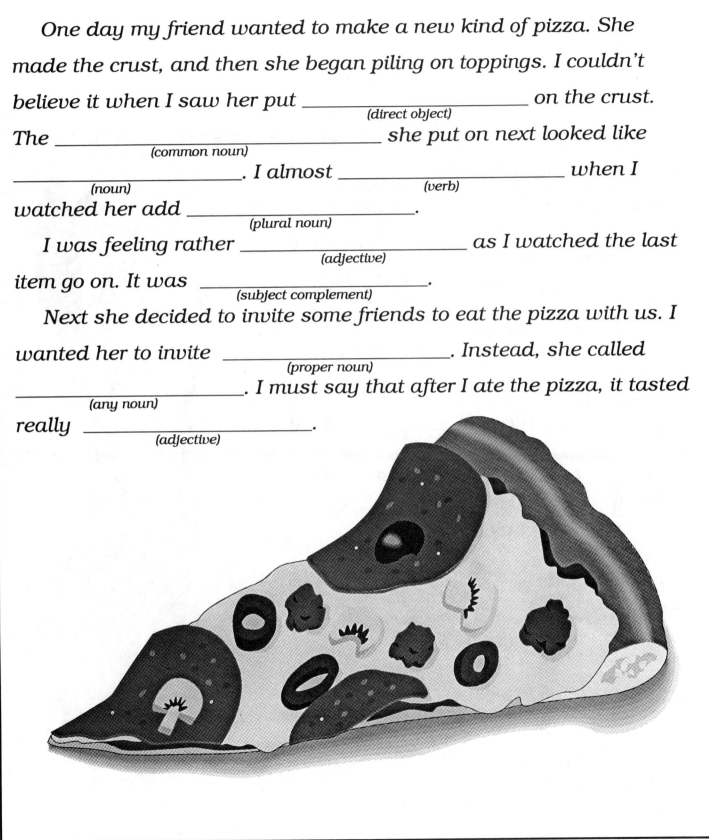

GA1497

Student Instructions: In each of the blank spaces write your choice of one or more words fitting the descriptions in parentheses.

The Substitute Teacher

Oh, no! _____ did not show up at school today.
(complete subject)

Someone said she _____.
(complete predicate)

Then our principal, _____, announced very
(proper noun)

_____ that we would have a substitute. When we
(adverb)

saw her, we almost _____. She
(intransitive verb)

looked _____ and
(adjective)

_____. I knew that I must
(adjective)

_____. But I was
(action verb)

_____.
(adjective)

The problem began when she asked

_____ to answer a question. "Why,"
(proper noun)

she began, "did the _____ always
(proper noun)

_____ in the _____?"
(action verb)   (object of preposition)

My friend didn't know _____.
(direct object)

"Your punishment will be to

_____ three times before
(action verb)

_____.
(object of preposition)

That punishment was simply

_____. I knew I had to
(predicate adjective)

_____ fast! So I
(action verb)

_____.
(complete predicate)

From then on I _____.
(complete predicate)

Grammar Pop-Up Cards

Several sets of grammar pop-up cards are provided later in this section. For preparation of these cards, please see pages 7-10.

Parts of a Sentence: Two pop-up sets involve the parts of a sentence. Level A has cards with the words **Subject** and **Predicate**. Instructional wording for this level may vary, but here is one possibility: "You have two cards on your desk. One has the word **Subject** and the other **Predicate**. (Review these concepts, if necessary.) I am going to show you a sentence with a section underlined. If the underlined part is the subject, hold up your card that has the word **Subject** on it. Hold up the card with the word **Predicate** if the underlined part is the predicate. Here is the first sentence. (Example: The young boy <u>crossed the street</u>.) Hold up one of your cards. (Allow time for students to answer.) That's right, the answer is **Predicate**. The next sentence is . . ."

Level B cards contain the items **Simple Subject**, **Simple Predicate**, **Complete Subject**, and **Complete Predicate**. This level may proceed in the same manner as described with Level A.

Types of Nouns: Pop-up cards for this concept contain the items **Common Nouns** and **Proper Nouns**. Here is one possible wording for the activity: "You have two cards on your desk. One has the words **Common Nouns** and the other one **Proper Nouns**. I am going to show you a word that will be either a common noun or a proper noun. The word is written with all capital letters so there will be no clues. If you think it is a common noun, please hold up the card with those two words on it. Do likewise if it is a proper noun. (Allow time for questions.) The first word is *TEXAS*. (Allow time for students to answer.) That's right, Texas. It is a proper noun because it is a specific place. The next word is *MARCH*. I'll bet you need to hear this in a sentence before you can get this one right. Okay: *On March 7 of last year . . .*"

Parts of Speech: Two levels of parts of speech pop-up cards are provided. Level A has **Noun**, **Pronoun**, **Verb**, and **Adjective**. Level B adds **Adverb**, **Preposition**, **Conjunction**, and **Interjection**.

Word Groups: Pop-up cards for this concept contain the items **Sentence**, **Fragment**, and **Run-on Sentence**. Here is one possible wording for the activity: "You have three cards on your desk. One has the word **Sentence**, one **Fragment**, and one **Run-on Sentence**. I am going to read a group of words to you. They will be either a complete sentence, a sentence fragment, or a run-on sentence. (If the sentences are shown, explain that a period will always be placed at the end—even though some will be sentence fragments. This is to eliminate clues for the answer, and it is because those who use sentence fragments in their writing almost always follow them with a period.) Hold up one of your cards to show which you think it is. (Allow time for questions.) The first group is *Early in the morning before the sun rises.* (Allow time for students to answer.) That's right, **Fragment** is the correct answer because it is not a complete sentence. Next is . . ."

Verb Tenses: Pop-up cards for the three verb tenses **Present**, **Past**, and **Future** are provided. Here is one possible wording for the activity: "You have three cards on your desk. One has the word **Present**, one **Past**, and one **Future**. I am going to read a sentence to you. Listen to this

GA1497

sentence to determine if the verb tense is present, past, or future. Hold up one of your cards to show which you think it is. (Allow time for questions.) The first sentence is *The lost little girl screamed for help*. (Allow time for answers.) That's right, **Past** (tense) is the correct answer because it has already happened and it is therefore in the past. Next is . . ."

Types of Sentences: Pop-up cards for the four types of sentences are provided. Here is one possible wording for the activity: "You have four cards on your desk. One has the word **Declarative**, one **Interrogative**, one **Imperative**, and one **Exclamatory**. I am going to read a sentence to you. Listen to this sentence to determine which type it might be. Hold up one of your cards to show which you think it is. (Allow time for questions.) The first sentence is *There's a huge monster standing behind you!* (Allow time for answers.) That's right, **Exclamatory** is the correct answer because of the strong feeling expressed. Next is . . ."

THERE'S A MONSTER STANDING BEHIND YOU!

Exclamatory

Uses of Nouns or Pronouns: Two levels of pop-up cards for nouns and pronouns are provided. Level A includes **Subject**, **Direct Object**, and **Object of the Preposition**. Level B adds the **Indirect Object** and the **Subject Complement**. Here is one possible wording for the Level B activity: "There are five cards on your desk. Each one states a use for a noun or pronoun in a sentence. I am going to show you a sentence with a noun or pronoun underlined. Study this sentence to determine the use of that noun or pronoun. Hold up one of your cards to show which you think it is. (Allow time for questions.) The first sentence is *Fred gave <u>me</u> the answer*. (Allow time for answers.) That's right, the pronoun *me* is the indirect object because it tells to whom something is being given—without using the word *to*. The next sentence is . . ."

Sentence Forms: Pop-up cards for four types of sentences are provided. Here is one possible wording for the activity: "You have four cards on your desk. Each one identifies a form of a sentence that we have studied in the past. I am going to read a sentence to you. Listen to this sentence to determine which type it might be. Hold up one of your cards to show which you think it is. (Allow time for questions.) The first sentence is: *My sister sings while my brother plays the piano*. (Allow time for answers.) That's right, **Complex** is the correct answer because it has one main clause that could be a sentence by itself *(my sister sings)* and one clause that could not be a sentence by itself *(while my brother plays the piano)*. The next sentence is . . ."

Sentences or word groups for the above sets of cards may be written on the chalkboard, on sentence strips (for small-group instruction), or on transparency film to be used with the overhead projector. Several starters for each of these categories are provided. An abundance of additional examples may be found in textbooks and workbooks.

84

GA1497

<u>Jill</u> laughed at him.

The baby <u>smiled</u>.

Where did <u>Bobby</u> go?

The proud, tall peacock <u>strutted back and forth</u>.

Starters for Parts of a Sentence: (Level B—Those in Level A may also be used with B.)

In the closet was my old <u>coat</u>.

<u>Go</u> home.

<u>Three fine young ladies</u> sang in the choir.

Dad <u>mowed the lawn yesterday</u>.

Starters for Types of Nouns:

LOOK AT THAT <u>TREE</u>.

IS <u>MARY</u> ASLEEP?

THAT <u>BOOK</u> WAS VERY SPECIAL.

Answers: subject, predicate, subject, predicate, simple subject, simple predicate, complete subject, complete predicate, common, proper, common

We wear white shoes.

We wear white shoes.

We wear white shoes.

We wear white shoes.

Wow! While in street clothes, he paced nervously!

Wow! While in street clothes, he paced nervously!

Wow! While in street clothes, he paced nervously!

Wow! While in street clothes, he paced nervously!

Wow! While in street clothes, he paced nervously!

Wow! While in street clothes, he paced nervously!

Wow! While in street clothes, he paced nervously!

Wow! While in street clothes, he paced nervously!

Answers: (A) pronoun, verb, adjective, noun; (B) interjection, conjunction, preposition, adjective, noun, pronoun, verb, adverb

GA1497

In the morning there will be presents for all.

Only fourteen of the men in all.

I'm tired I haven't slept for days.

Because Bob was sick.

Sue helped me she likes me.

Go home.

I always wash dishes for my mom.

We watched as the flames died down.

No one will see you there.

The giant went to sleep.

I shall return.

Everybody watches cartoons.

Answers: sentence, fragment, run-on sentence, fragment, run-on sentence, sentence, present, past, future, past, future, present

I enjoy playing baseball.

What time is it?

No! The building is on fire!

Run to first base.

Who ate my lunch?

Bring me a sandwich.

Starters for Uses of Nouns or Pronouns: (Level A)

<u>Fred</u> threw the ball to me.

Fred threw the <u>ball</u> to me.

Fred threw the ball to <u>me</u>.

Make my <u>day</u>!

We walked to <u>school</u>.

Is <u>Bill</u> reading the newspaper?

Answers: declarative, interrogative, exclamatory, imperative, interrogative, imperative,
subject, direct object, object of preposition, direct object, object of preposition, subject

GA1497

Before noon <u>we</u> need to leave.

Jane dropped the <u>glass</u>.

It fell to the <u>floor</u>.

Give <u>me</u> more money.

He is my <u>coach</u>.

Send <u>Sam</u> the library book.

You're the greatest <u>mom</u> in the world!

Starters for Sentence Forms:

Birds fly.

Mom cooks and Dad washes dishes.

We hiked because we felt great.

If Ed wins, I lose and Ann stays.

Ted and Jane went home and ate dinner.

Answers: subject, direct object, object of preposition, indirect object, subject complement, indirect object, subject complement, simple, compound, complex, compound-complex, simple

GA1497

See page 10 for preparation instructions.

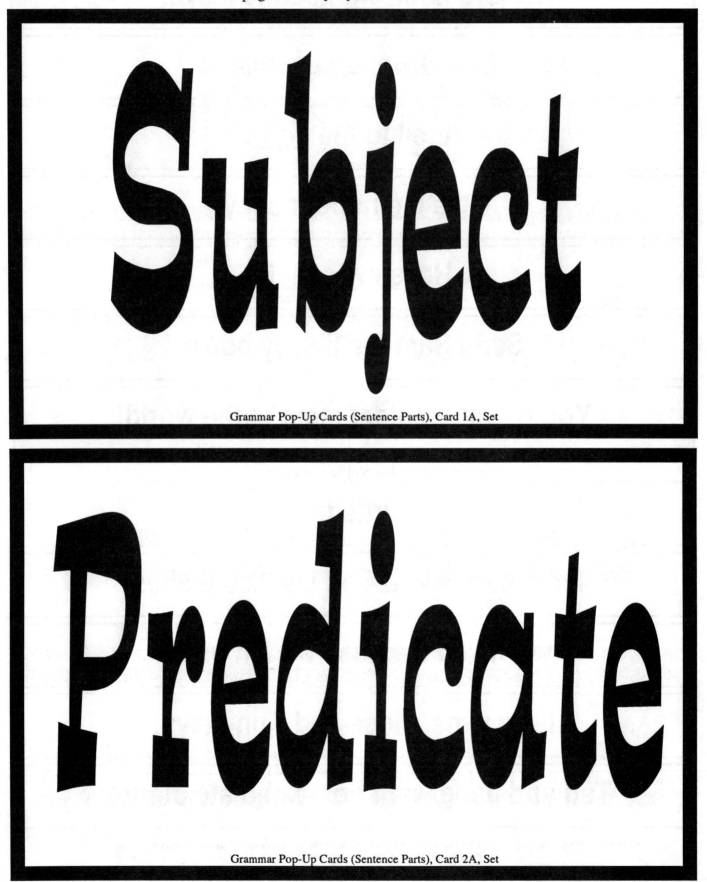

Grammar Pop-Up Cards (Sentence Parts), Card 1A, Set

Grammar Pop-Up Cards (Sentence Parts), Card 2A, Set

GA1497

Cards for Grammar Pop-Up: Sentence Parts (Level B)

See page 10 for preparation instructions.

Simple Subject

Grammar Pop-Up Cards (Sentence Parts), Card 1B, Set

Complete Subject

Grammar Pop-Up Cards (Sentence Parts), Card 2B, Set

Simple Predicate

Grammar Pop-Up Cards (Sentence Parts), Card 3B, Set

Complete Predicate

Grammar Pop-Up Cards (Sentence Parts), Card 4B, Set

GA1497

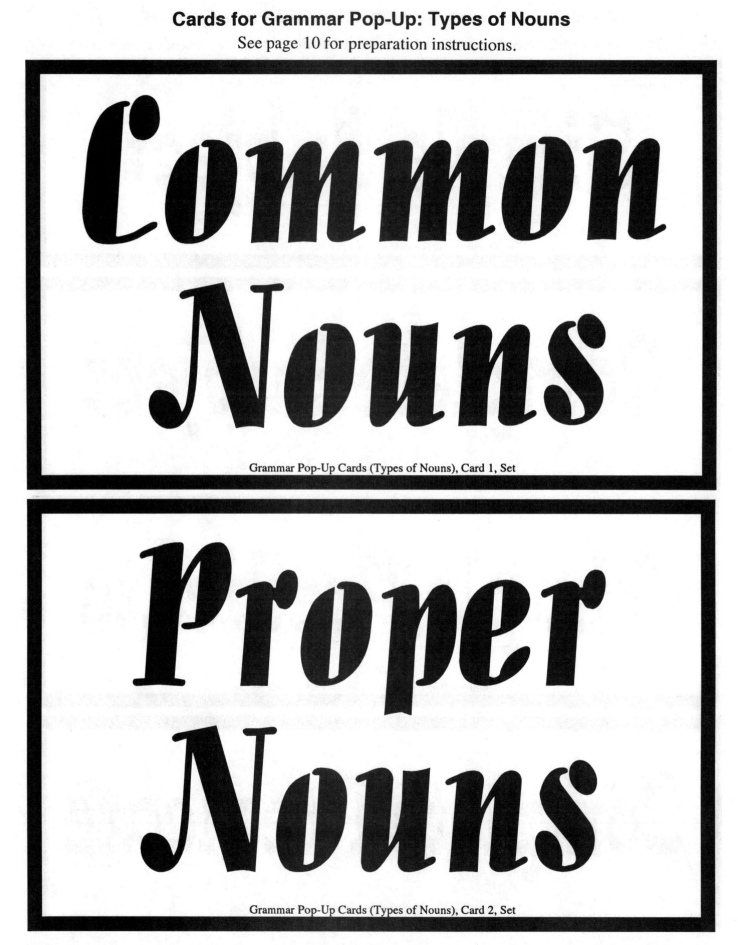

Common Nouns

Grammar Pop-Up Cards (Types of Nouns), Card 1, Set

Proper Nouns

Grammar Pop-Up Cards (Types of Nouns), Card 2, Set

GA1497

Cards for Grammar Pop-Up: Parts of Speech (Level A)

See page 10 for preparation instructions.

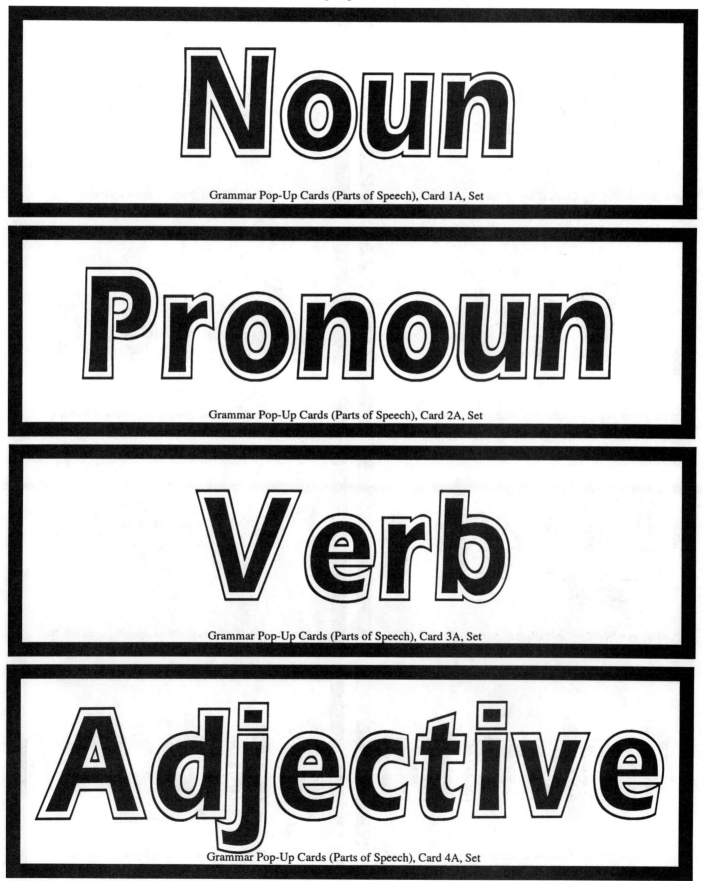

Noun

Grammar Pop-Up Cards (Parts of Speech), Card 1A, Set

Pronoun

Grammar Pop-Up Cards (Parts of Speech), Card 2A, Set

Verb

Grammar Pop-Up Cards (Parts of Speech), Card 3A, Set

Adjective

Grammar Pop-Up Cards (Parts of Speech), Card 4A, Set

GA1497

Cards for Grammar Pop-Up: Parts of Speech (Level B)

See page 10 for preparation instructions.

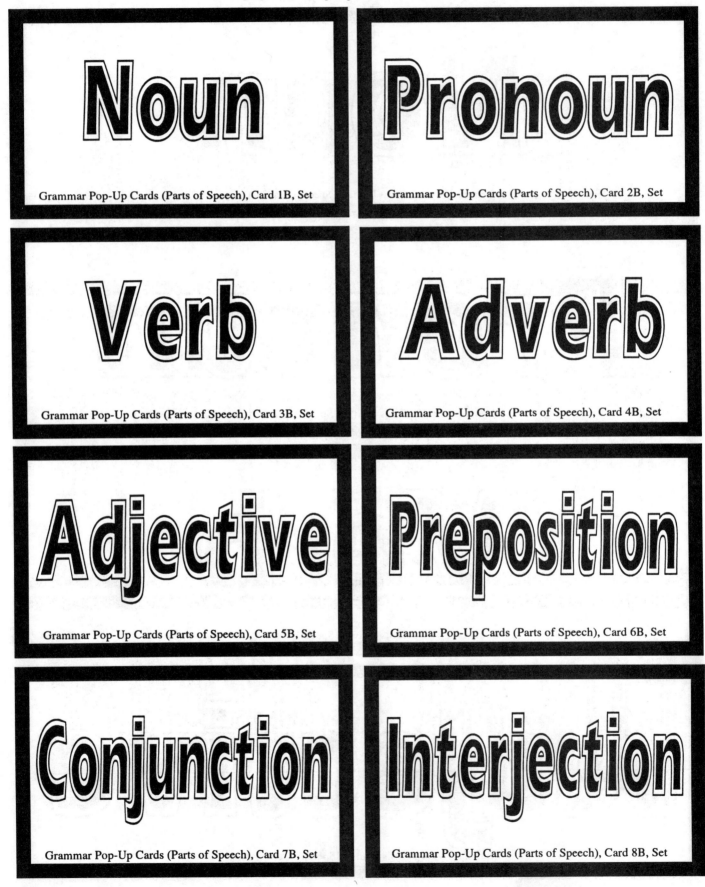

Noun

Grammar Pop-Up Cards (Parts of Speech), Card 1B, Set

Pronoun

Grammar Pop-Up Cards (Parts of Speech), Card 2B, Set

Verb

Grammar Pop-Up Cards (Parts of Speech), Card 3B, Set

Adverb

Grammar Pop-Up Cards (Parts of Speech), Card 4B, Set

Adjective

Grammar Pop-Up Cards (Parts of Speech), Card 5B, Set

Preposition

Grammar Pop-Up Cards (Parts of Speech), Card 6B, Set

Conjunction

Grammar Pop-Up Cards (Parts of Speech), Card 7B, Set

Interjection

Grammar Pop-Up Cards (Parts of Speech), Card 8B, Set

GA1497

Cards for Grammar Pop-Up: Word Groups
See page 10 for preparation instructions.

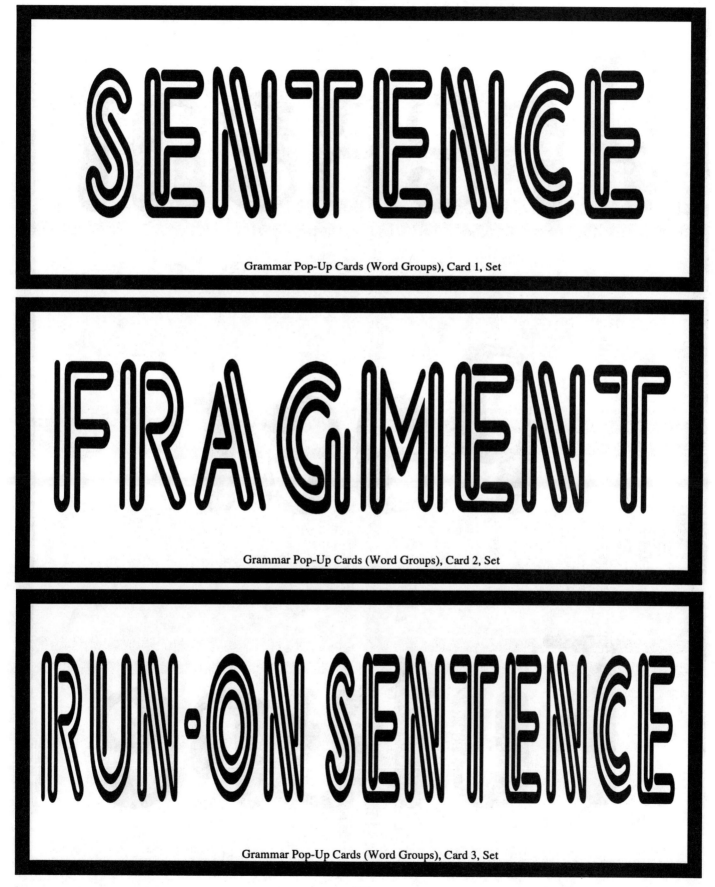

SENTENCE

Grammar Pop-Up Cards (Word Groups), Card 1, Set

FRAGMENT

Grammar Pop-Up Cards (Word Groups), Card 2, Set

RUN-ON SENTENCE

Grammar Pop-Up Cards (Word Groups), Card 3, Set

GA1497

Cards for Grammar Pop-Up: Verb Tenses

See page 10 for preparation instructions.

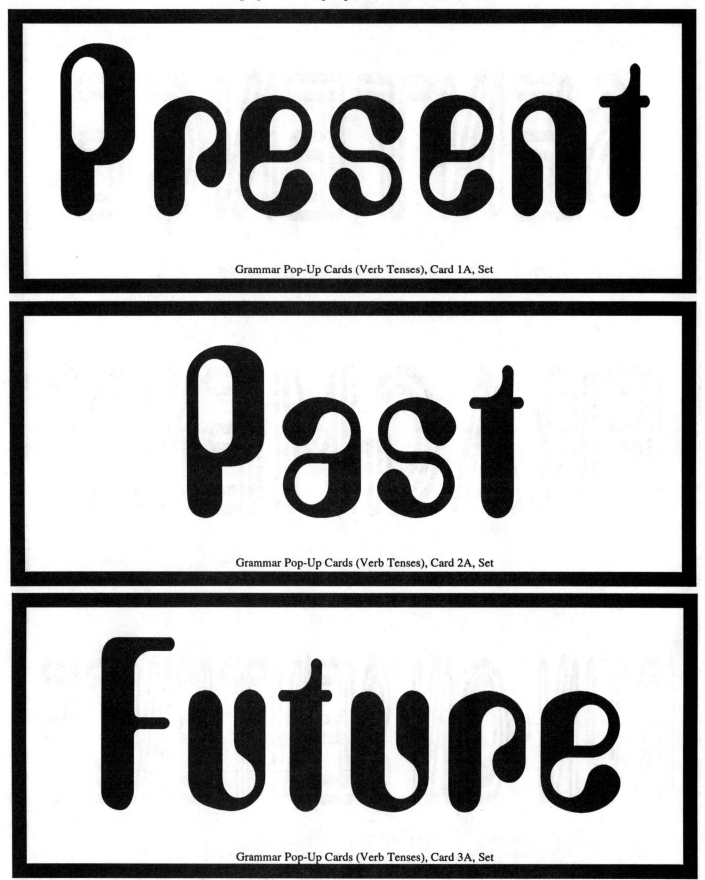

Present

Grammar Pop-Up Cards (Verb Tenses), Card 1A, Set

Past

Grammar Pop-Up Cards (Verb Tenses), Card 2A, Set

Future

Grammar Pop-Up Cards (Verb Tenses), Card 3A, Set

GA1497

Cards for Grammar Pop-Up: Types of Sentences

See page 10 for preparation instructions.

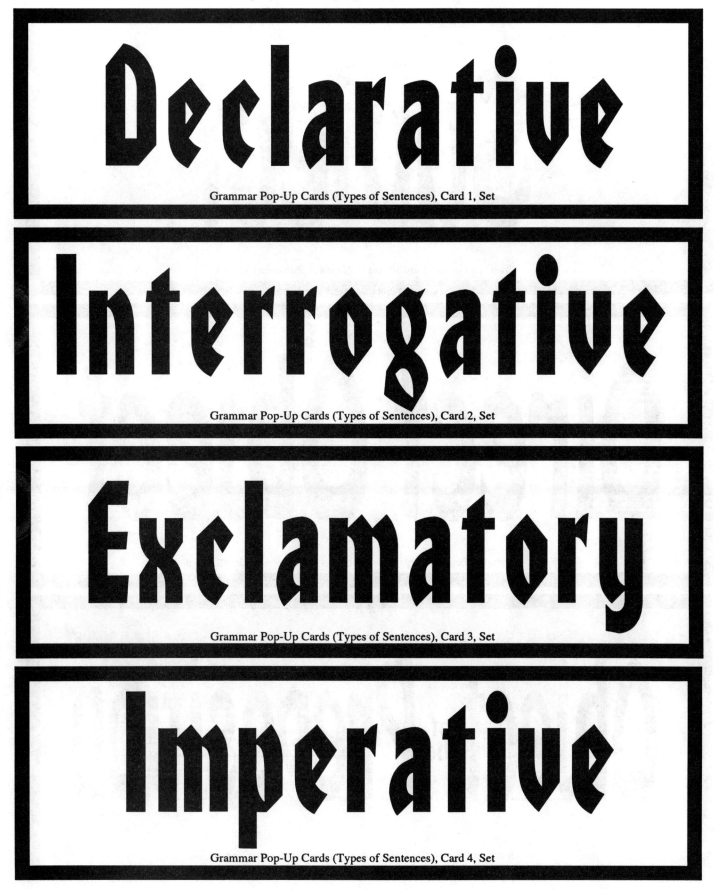

Declarative

Grammar Pop-Up Cards (Types of Sentences), Card 1, Set

Interrogative

Grammar Pop-Up Cards (Types of Sentences), Card 2, Set

Exclamatory

Grammar Pop-Up Cards (Types of Sentences), Card 3, Set

Imperative

Grammar Pop-Up Cards (Types of Sentences), Card 4, Set

GA1497

Cards for Grammar Pop-Up: Uses of Nouns or Pronouns (Level A)

See page 10 for preparation instructions.

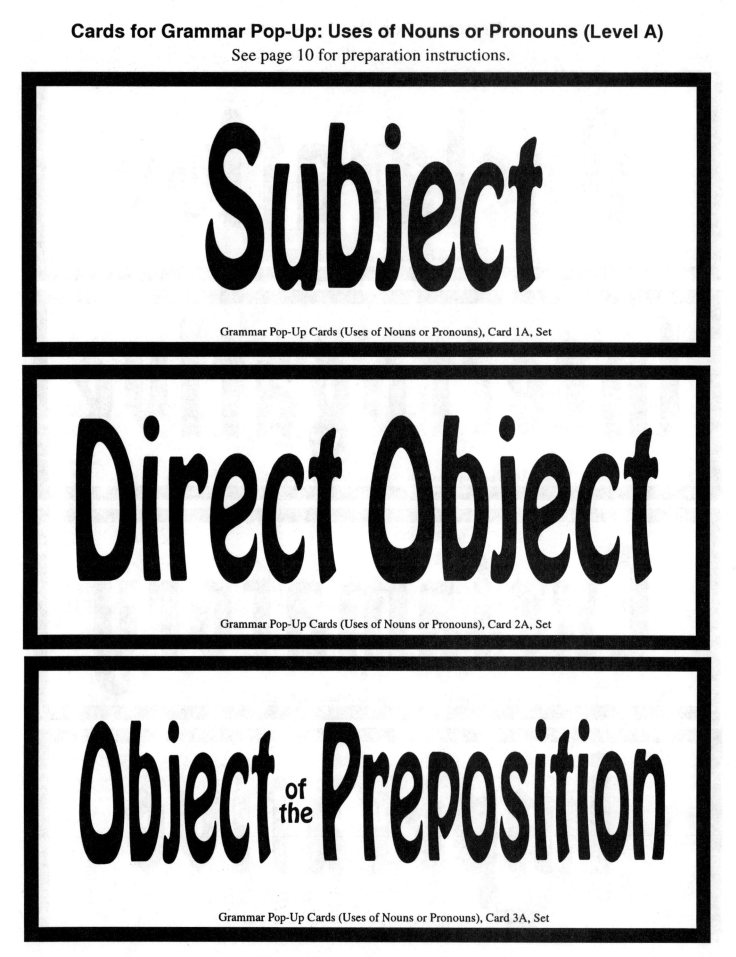

Subject

Grammar Pop-Up Cards (Uses of Nouns or Pronouns), Card 1A, Set

Direct Object

Grammar Pop-Up Cards (Uses of Nouns or Pronouns), Card 2A, Set

Object of the Preposition

Grammar Pop-Up Cards (Uses of Nouns or Pronouns), Card 3A, Set

Cards for Grammar Pop-Up: Uses of Nouns or Pronouns (Level B)

See page 10 for preparation instructions.

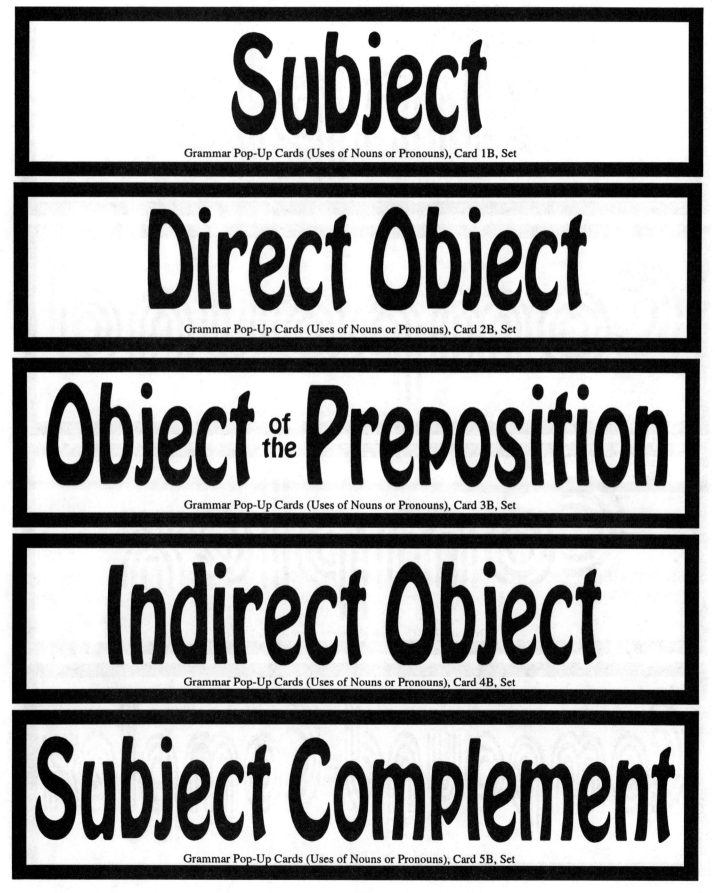

Subject

Grammar Pop-Up Cards (Uses of Nouns or Pronouns), Card 1B, Set

Direct Object

Grammar Pop-Up Cards (Uses of Nouns or Pronouns), Card 2B, Set

Object of the Preposition

Grammar Pop-Up Cards (Uses of Nouns or Pronouns), Card 3B, Set

Indirect Object

Grammar Pop-Up Cards (Uses of Nouns or Pronouns), Card 4B, Set

Subject Complement

Grammar Pop-Up Cards (Uses of Nouns or Pronouns), Card 5B, Set

GA1497

Cards for Grammar Pop-Up: Sentence Forms
See page 10 for preparation instructions.

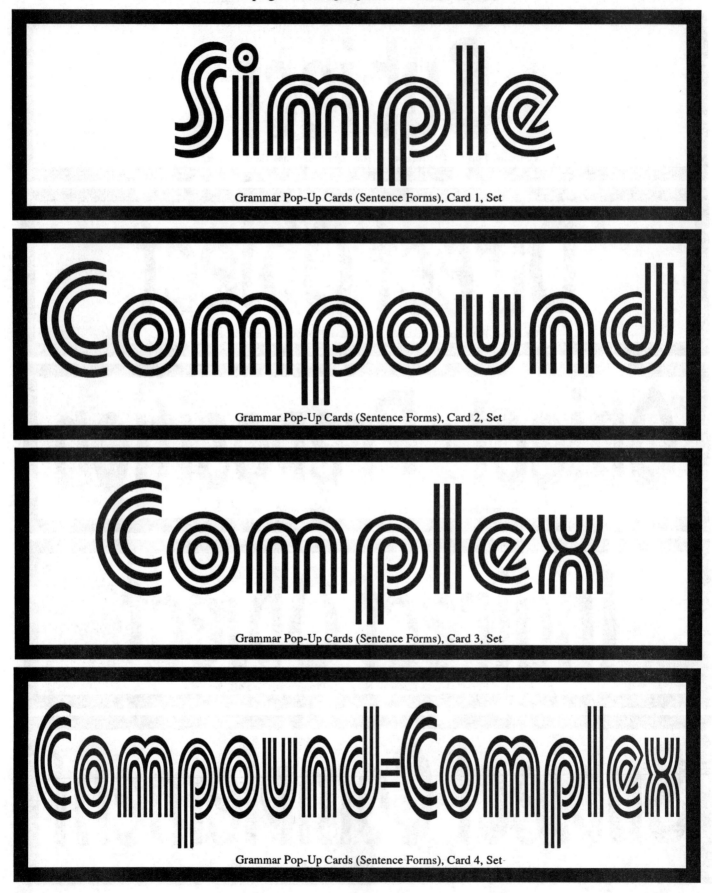

Grammar Pop-Up Cards (Sentence Forms), Card 1, Set

Grammar Pop-Up Cards (Sentence Forms), Card 2, Set

Grammar Pop-Up Cards (Sentence Forms), Card 3, Set

Grammar Pop-Up Cards (Sentence Forms), Card 4, Set

GA1497

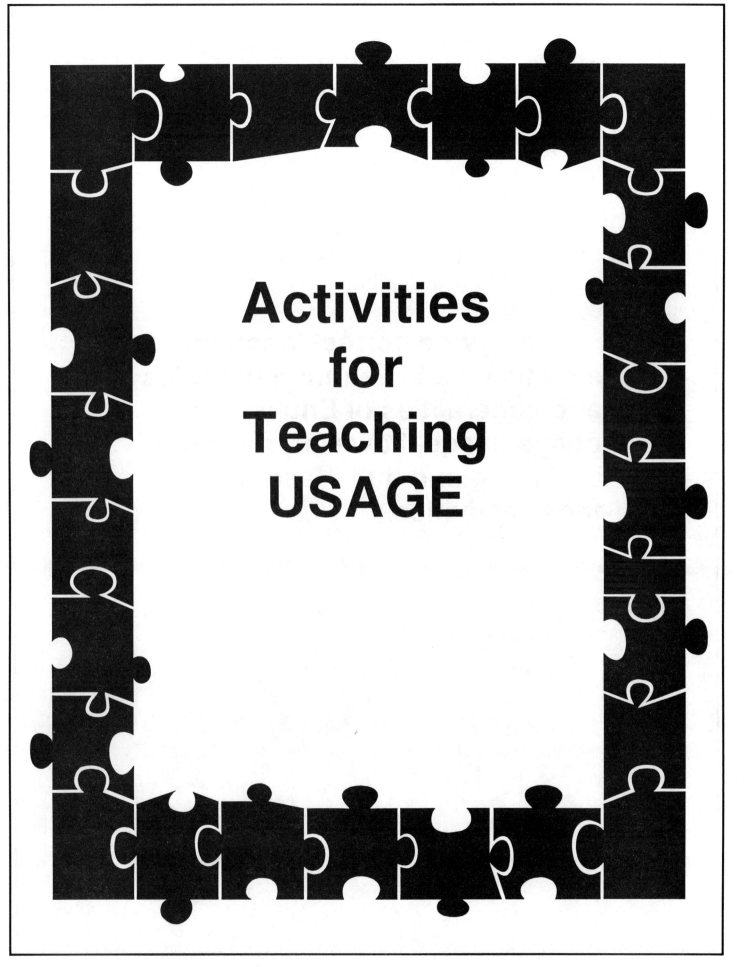

Activities
for
Teaching
USAGE

GA1497

Observing correct language is a lifetime task. Learning the rules and generalities of English language usage, however, need not be boring and dull. Have fun with these activities.

Usage Fill-In Fun

Please read pages 11-12 for complete information regarding the intent, use, and preparation of the Fill-In Fun Activities contained in this book.

Samples Provided for Usage Skills: On pages 104-106 are three samples of Fill-In Fun activities for usage skills. "What Was It?" may be used to help teach the correct choices of *I* or *me* and *saw* or *seen*. "Big Bull's Trip" asks students to choose correctly between *rode* or *ridden* and *drove* or *driven*. "The Strange Visitor" tackles two pairs of words that are very frequently misused even by educated adults. These pairs are *sit* or *set* and *lie* or *lay*. This page includes many forms of both of these confusing verbs (*lie, lay, lain, lying; lay, laid, laying; sit, sat,* and *set*).

Preparing Additional Usage Fill-In Fun Pages: Examine the usage material in the language arts textbooks and workbooks for your grade level. Consider turning some of these materials into Usage Fill-In Fun for your students.

Answers for Provided Usage Fill-In Fun:

"What Was It?": One day Joe and I were walking down the street. All of a sudden we saw a very strange creature. Never in my life had I ever seen such a character before. It approached Joe and me very slowly. It looked at us very curiously. Perhaps it hadn't ever seen folks who looked like Joe and me. By then I had seen enough. The character saw us run home. When I woke up the next morning, I was not sure whether or not I really had seen such a creature at all!

"Big Bull's Trip": Big Bull was grazing in the pasture one day when his owner, Mr. Mack, drove up and said, "I think it's time Big Bull went on a trip."
"Oh, boy!" thought Big Bull. "I've always wanted to go on a vacation, and I have never ridden in Mr. Mack's truck." So Big Bull packed his suitcase.
Soon Mr. Mack drove up again in a large truck and loaded Big Bull into the back. After they had ridden for awhile, Big Bull said, "I like this! I have never before ridden in a truck this large."
Before long Mr. Mack had driven almost ninety miles. Big Bull was exhausted. "If I had known we would have ridden this far, I'd have brought some food!"
Big Bull wondered if Mr. Mack hadn't driven far enough.
Mr. Mack drove the last few miles, then he stopped at a large building. After he had driven Big Bull inside, he wondered if Big Bull had read the words on the outside of that large building. What do you think they said?

"The Strange Visitor": Last night as I lay in bed pretending to be asleep, I saw a skeleton walk in and sit down at my computer. He laid his books on the floor, then he set the telephone receiver on his bony shoulder. I had lain there only a few minutes when he dialed 1-800-GHOST. I quickly sat up in bed. I tried to lie back down, but I couldn't. There he sat for several hours without ever laying the receiver down. I sat silently and watched.
Boldly I asked, "Who are you? And why are you sitting at my computer?"
He looked at me and said, "I'm a ghostwriter." Then he disappeared, never to return again. Now as I lie in . . . .

GA1497

Student Instructions: In each of the blank spaces write the correct word from the choices in parentheses.

What Was It?

One day Joe and _____ were walking down the street. All of a
(I me)

sudden we _____ a very strange creature. Never in my life had
(saw seen)

_____ ever _____ such a
(I me)   (saw seen)

character before. It approached

Joe and _____ very slowly. It
(I me)

looked at us very curiously.

Perhaps it hadn't ever

_____ folks
(saw seen)

who looked like

Joe and _____.
(I me)

By then I had

_____ enough.
(saw seen)

The character

_____ us run
(saw seen)

home. When I

woke up the next

morning, I was not

sure whether or not

I really had

_____ such a
(saw seen)

creature at all!

GA1497

Student Instructions: In each of the blank spaces write the correct word from the choices in parentheses.

Big Bull's Trip

Big Bull was grazing in the pasture one day when his owner, Mr. Mack, _____ up and said, "I think it's time Big Bull went on a
(drove driven)
trip."

"Oh, boy!" thought Big Bull. "I've always wanted to go on a vacation, and I have never _____ in Mr. Mack's truck." So Big
(rode ridden)
Bull packed his suitcase.

Soon Mr. Mack _____ up again in a large truck and loaded
(drive drove)
Big Bull into the back. After they had _____ for awhile, Big Bull
(rode ridden)
said, "I like this! I have never before _____ in a truck this large."
(rode ridden)

Before long Mr. Mack had _____ almost ninety miles. Big Bull
(drove driven)
was exhausted. "If I had known we would have _____ this
(rode ridden)
far, I'd have brought some food!"

Big Bull wondered if Mr. Mack hadn't _____ far enough.
(drove driven)

Mr. Mack _____ the last
(drove driven)
few miles, then he stopped at a large building. After he had

_____ Big Bull inside, he
(drove driven)
wondered if Big Bull had read the words on the outside of that large building. What do you think they said?

GA1497

Student Instructions: In each of the blank spaces write the correct word from the choices in parentheses.

The Strange Visitor

Last night as I _____ in bed pretending to be asleep, I saw a
(laid lay)

skeleton walk in and _____ down at my computer. He _____ his
(sit set) (laid lay)

books on the floor, then he _____ the telephone receiver on his bony
(set sat)

shoulder. I had _____ there only a few minutes when he dialed
(laid lain)

1-800-GHOST. I quickly _____ up in bed. I tried to _____ back
(set sat) (lay lie)

down, but I couldn't. There he _____ for several hours without
(sat set)

ever _____ the receiver down. I _____ silently and watched.
(laying lying) (sat set)

Boldly I asked, "Who are you? And why are you _____ at
(sitting setting)

my computer?"

He looked at me and said, "I'm a ghost-

writer." Then he disappeared,

never to return again.

Now as I _____ in bed
(lie lay)
each night, I wonder

what happened

to him. I also

wonder

what it

means to

be a

ghostwriter.

Do you know?

106

GA1497

"Tense Talk" (Correct Verbs)

One of the most frequently made errors in language mechanics, not only by young learners but by adults as well, is the incorrect choice of verb tense. A problem in teaching this skill in elementary and middle schools seems to be that the exercises are generally on-paper experiences rather than oral language activities. **Hearing** the correct verb forms aids in the future use of the appropriate choice, whether in writing or speaking. The purpose of Tense Talk, therefore, is to give students an opportunity to hear and use (orally) correct verb tenses.

Classroom Procedures: Divide the class equally into Team A and Team B. One team forms a line on one side of the room, and the other team forms a line on the opposite side.

The first member of Team A gives the present form of any verb in the following context: *Today I _____.* (Should the selected verb be transitive, a direct object may follow. Additional context of any type is encouraged.)

The first member of Team B repeats the present tense context, then adds the past and past participial forms in the contexts of: *Yesterday I _____ . And I have _____ many times before.* An example of a response from Team B might be: *Today I sit in my chair. Yesterday I sat in my chair. I have sat in my chair many times before.*

After hearing this response, the Team A member indicates whether or not the responses are correct. (The teacher will need to listen carefully to make this judgment accurately.) If the answer is not correct, the Team B member sits down and the next member in line for Team B responds to

the same present tense context. This process continues (with inappropriate responders sitting down) until someone on the team gives a completely correct answer or until the entire team has been seated. In case of the latter, Team A is declared the winner.

When a completely correct answer is given (both past and past participial forms are correct), that team member then goes to the end of the line, and the next member in line for that same team gives the present form of a new verb—with the same context—to a new member of the opposite team.

After giving a response, every team member will do one of two things: sit down if the answer is incorrect, or go to the end of the line if the answer is correct.

Several adaptations of this activity may be made. If the teacher chooses, the team members who give incorrect responses may have three chances before actually having to sit down. (For the first incorrect response, say, "That's a 'J' on you." The next time, it's an "O," and the last time a "Y." At that point the student must sit. This allows for three errors in all.)

Instead of the winning team needing to seat the entire opposing team, the team with the higher number of members standing after a previously determined number of minutes have passed is declared the winner.

Do not allow any discussion while the team members are thinking through their answers. This will help promote better listening and thinking skills. After each individual verb has been used, any amount of entire group discussion may occur.

Some starter words you might communicate to some of the team members during the first few trial rounds of the activity are as follows: *lie, lay, lain; sit, sat, sat; awake, awoke, awaked or awoken; dive, dove or dived, dived; sneak, sneaked, sneaked; drag, dragged, dragged; arise, arose, arisen; go, went, gone; lay, laid, laid; set, set, set; awaken, awakened, awakened; baby-sit, baby-sat, baby-sat; shoe, shod, shod; cost, cost, cost; is (be, am, are), was, been; shear, sheared, sheared or shorn; put, put, put*; or *run, ran, run.* Check your language arts textbooks for others appropriate for your grade level.

After a few rounds of this activity, encourage the students to try to find some "seaters" that will cause the entire opposing team to sit down. This encouragement may help students investigate their dictionaries, their "older" friends, etc. (One "seater" a fourth-grade student found was *methinks.* This verb has the past tense of *methought*, but it has no past participial form. Correct answer: *Today methinks the plan is good. Yesterday methought the plan was good. There is no other verb form for this word.* It can be an entire team seater and also an interesting word to study.) Allow students to use any list they have prepared only while they are giving their present tense form, but not while they are responding to the opposing team. Note that this is also a listening activity, for when students miss either the past tense or past participial form of the verb, those who have listened will have clues regarding which responses might not be entirely correct. For example, consider the following dialog:

Kevin (Team A): Today I **lie** down for a nap.
Paula (Team B): Today I **lie** down for a nap. Yesterday I **laid** down for a nap. I have **laid** down for a nap many times before.
Kevin (Team A): That is not correct. (Paula is then seated. Dustin is now at the front of the Team B line.)
Dustin (Team B): Today I **lie** down for a nap. Yesterday I **lay** down for a nap. I have **laid** down for a nap many times before.
Kevin (Team A): That is not correct. (Dustin is then seated. Ann is now at the front of the Team B line.)
Ann (Team B): Today I **lie** down for a nap. Yesterday I **laid** down for a nap. I have **lain** down for a nap many times before.
Kevin (Team A): That is not correct. (Ann is then seated. Ed is now at the front of the Team B line.)
Ed (Team B): Today I **lie** down for a nap. Yesterday I **laid** down for a nap. I have **laid** down for a nap many times before.
Kevin (Team A): That is not correct. You must have been sleeping, for that is the same answer Paula gave. (Ed is then seated. Susan is now at the front of the Team B line.)
Susan (Team B): Today I **lie** down for a nap. Yesterday I **lay** down for a nap. I have **lain** down for a nap many times before.
Kevin (Team A): Wow! That is correct! (Susan walks to the end of the line for Team B.)
Michelle (Team B): Today I **dive** into the water.
Kevin (Team A): Today I **dive** into the water. Yesterday I **dove** into the water. I have **dove** into the water many times before.
Michelle (Team B): Not correct! (Kevin sits down. Lee is now at the front of the Team A line.)
Lee (Team A): Today I **dive** into the water. Yesterday I **dove** into the water. I have **dived** into the water many times before.
Michelle (Team B): You got it! Actually either **dived** or **dove** can be used as the past tense, but only **dived** is the correct word for the last sentence. (Lee walks to the end of the line for Team A.)
Robbie (Team A): Today I **baby-sit** for my neighbor . . .

It is amazing how this oral activity can train the ear (and eventually the pen) to produce better choices of verb tenses. One of the most outstanding traits of this activity (according to both students and teachers) is that there are no papers to grade. It can be used when only a few minutes of class time remain, when only a few students are in the classroom, every Tuesday morning, etc. It works!

Granny's Grammar Game

Students often think that writing correctly is old-fashioned. "That's the way my granny would talk," they'll say. This comment inspired Granny's Grammar Game, an activity to help develop better usage skills in serious writing.

Classroom procedures: Create a sentence that contains several grammatical "errors." Write this sentence on the chalkboard in view of all learners. Have previously arranged groups of students collectively decide what these errors might be. As a group, they write a list of these mistakes. When all groups have completed their lists, one member from each team will write this list on the chalkboard. After all writers have returned to their groups, these lists may be checked and discussed. The following illustration shows a chalkboard with a target sentence and group responses:

Sentence:
Their wasn't hardly no room to set on the bench after the dog had already laid down.

Group A Changes:
✓ No to any
✓ sit to set

Group B Changes:
✓ Their to there
✓ wasn't to was
✓ no to any
✓ set to sit
✓ laid to lain
(The winner!)

Group C changes:
✓ their to there
✓ no to any
✗ laid to lay

Each prepared sentence would need to meet the needs of the grade levels of the learners involved. The following are some possibilities:

- Everyone in both classes have their projects for Jerry and I to except. (*have* should be *has, their* should be *his/her, I* should be *me,* and *except* should be *accept*)
- Neither the managers or the coach of the teams want they're players to lay in the sun. (*or* should be *nor, want* should be *wants, they're* should be *their,* and *lay* should be *lie*)
- Tom did not feel bad about his leaving. (There are no errors in this sentence. That's sneaky!)

GA1497

Granny's Grammar Game Adaptation: An adaptation of this activity involves asking each team **only one question** about grammar. The team discusses the question until they reach the point where each team member is able to explain the answer and why that answer is the right choice. The instructional leader may call on **any member** of the group to give the answer. This becomes strong encouragement for each member to be able to vocalize the right answer, and for the "smart" students to make sure everyone in the group knows both the answer and the reasoning behind it. A score can be kept, if desired. An example of a question is, "What is the subject of the sentence *In the meadow was an injured bird*"? Any number of individual questions may be posed to these groups. The actual sentences or language items may be taken from the textbook or workbook. When desired, groups with a predetermined number of correct responses may be rewarded by being exempted from homework for one day, etc.

Some starter sentences for this adaptation are:

- What is the simple subject in the following sentence? *Jack climbed the beanstalk.* (Jack)
- What type of sentence is the following? *Where are my books?* (Interrogative)
- What mark of punctuation should be at the end of this sentence? *This building is on fire!* (Exclamation mark)
- Does the following sentence have an incorrect verb choice? *He set on the floor too long.* (Yes, *set* should be *sat*.)
- Does the following sentence contain a prepositional phrase? *I went to town yesterday.* If so, what is it? (Yes, it is *to town*.)
- What verb tense is used in the following sentence? *I will be absent tomorrow.* (Future tense)

Granny's Bonus Quiz: After a long and perhaps grueling practice period, reward your students by giving them the quiz below. The instructions are to circle a correct answer within each set of parentheses. Actually, either choice is accurate, depending upon the desired meaning. Therefore, every student who circles at least one choice in each case will have a perfect score, no matter which words are chosen. How nice to earn a perfect score, especially in language class!

The Language Quiz

Circle a correct choice of words within each set of parentheses:
1. Will anyone sing (beside, besides) me?
2. Sam gave Betty a higher score than (I, me).
3. Are you writing (to, two) boys?
4. (Their, There) cars were towed away.
5. The gift was (stationary, stationery).
6. (Weave, We've) only three stitches.
7. He told me to take two servings, but I didn't want (to, two).
8. John couldn't eat at the booth in the diner because of the (tacks, tax).

9 and 10. (Toe, Tow) the (line, lion).

Never forget that grammar study should not only be fun, exciting, and challenging, but it should also be rewarding!

GA1497

Usage Pop-Up Cards

Several sets of usage pop-up cards are provided later in this section. For preparation and general use of these cards, please read carefully pages 7-10.

The preparation of the usage pop-up cards will differ slightly from the general explanation and from those previously explained. One main difference involves the organization and storage of the cards. Rather than filing by sets of eighty-one different cards, file with sets of identical cards. For example, all the **a** cards should be filed together, all the **an** cards, all the **the** cards, all the **is** cards, all the **are** cards, etc. When you are ready for a pop-up exercise involving the correct choice of **is** or **are**, for instance, you can then pull both envelopes and distribute one of each of the cards to every student. Eighty-one envelopes will therefore be needed if all cards are prepared.

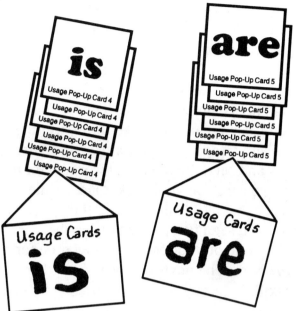

The usage pop-up cards provided on pages 122-130 represent several different areas of language development. The following are the general categories of these common usage problems.

Correct Choices of Articles: The three pop-up cards **a**, **an**, and **the** may be used to teach this usage choice. (These are Usage Pop-Up Cards 1-3.) Most teachers begin with just the **a** and **an** cards and later add **the**. Instructional wording for this concept may vary, but here is one possibility: "You have two cards on your desk. One has the word **a** and the other **an**. I am going to say a word and I want you to hold up the **a** card if you would say **a** in front of that word. For example, if I hold up the word *car*, since you would say *a car* instead of *an car*, you would hold up the card that has **a** on it. If I said the word *uncle*, since you would say *an uncle* instead of *a uncle*, you would hold up the card that has **an** on it. The first word is *apple*. Hold up one of your cards. (Allow time for answers.) That's right, the answer is **an**. We would say *an apple*. The next word is . . ."

Correct Choices of Singular or Plural Verbs: Eight pop-up cards are provided for this usage skill. These are **is**, **are**, **was**, **were**, **seems**, **seem**, **doesn't**, and **don't**. (These are Usage Pop-Up Cards 4-11.) In most cases students would deal with these in pairs, such as **don't** and **doesn't**. Instructional wording for this concept may vary, but here is one possibility: "You have two cards on your desk. One has the word **don't** and the other has the word **doesn't**. I am going to show you a sentence that has a blank space. If the word **don't** would fit into that space, please hold up that card. If the word **doesn't** fits, please hold up that card. The first sentence is *He _____ like my dress*. Hold up one of your cards. (Allow time for answers.) That's right, the answer is **doesn't**. *He doesn't like my dress*. The next sentence is . . ." Proceed likewise with your choice of the other word pairs for this skill.

GA1497

Correct Choices of Pronouns: Twelve pop-up cards are provided for this usage skill. These are **I, me, we, us, she, her, he, him, they, them, who,** and **whom.** (These are Usage Pop-Up Cards 12-23.) In most cases students would deal with these in pairs, such as **I** and **me.** Instructional wording for this concept may vary, but here is one possibility: "You have two cards on your desk. One has the word **I** and the other **me.** I am going to show you a sentence that has a blank space. If the word **I** would fit into that space, please hold up that card. If the word **me** fits, please hold up that card. The first sentence is *Jerry and _____ played basketball.* Hold up one of your cards. (Allow time for answers.) That's right, the answer is **I.** *Jerry and I played basketball.* The next sentence is . . ." Proceed likewise with your choices of other word pairs for this skill.

Correct Choices of Verb Tense: Fourteen pop-up cards are provided for this usage skill. These are **saw, seen, ran, run, did, done, went, gone, began, begun, knew, known, rode,** and **ridden.** (These are Usage Pop-Up Cards 24-37.) In most cases students would deal with these in pairs, such as **saw** and **seen.** Instructional wording for this concept may vary, but here is one possibility: "You have two cards on your desk. One has the word **saw** and the other **seen.** I am going to show you a sentence that has a blank space. If the word **saw** would fit into that space, please hold up that card. If the word **seen** fits, please hold up that card. The first sentence is *He _____ my report card.* Hold up one of your cards. (Allow time for answers.) That's right, the answer is **saw.** *He saw my report card.* The next sentence is . . ." Proceed likewise with your choices of other word pairs for this skill.

Correct Choices of Frequently Misused Verbs: Eleven pop-up cards are provided for this usage skill. These are **can, may, set, sit, sat, lie, lay, lain, laid, teach,** and **learn.** (These are Usage Pop-Up Cards 38-48.) In most cases students would deal with these in pairs, such as **can** and **may.** Instructional wording for this concept may vary, but here is one possibility: "You have two cards on your desk. One has the word **can** and the other **may.** I am going to show you a sentence that has a blank space. If the word **can** would fit into that space, please hold up that card. If the word **may** fits, please hold up that card. The first sentence is *Ask your teacher if you _____ leave the room.* Hold up one of your cards. (Allow time for answers.) That's right, the answer is **may.** *Ask your teacher if you **may** leave the room.* The next sentence is . . ." Proceed likewise with your choices of other word pairs for this skill.

Appropriate Spellings of Homophones and Possessives: Seventeen pop-up cards are provided for this usage skill. These are **its, it's, your, you're, their, there, they're, who's, whose, to, too, two, no, know, new, here,** and **hear**—plus Usage Pop-Up Card 34, **knew,** (to serve as one in the pair with **new**). (These are Usage Pop-Up Cards 49-65.) In most cases students would deal with these in pairs, such as **its** and **it's.** Instructional wording for this concept may vary, but here is one possibility: "You have two cards on your desk. One has the word **its** and the other **it's.** I am going to read a sentence to you that has the word **its/it's.** If the choice **i-t-s** is the one you would write if you were putting this sentence on paper, please hold up that card. If the choice **i-t-'-s** is the correct one, please hold up that card. The first sentence is *The bird hurt _____ wing.* Hold up one of your cards. (Allow time for answers.) That's right, the answer is **i-t-s.** The word is possessive instead of standing for the words *it is.* The next sentence is . . ." (See next page for illustration.) Proceed likewise with your choice of the other word pairs for this skill. Note that the first nine words selected pertain to pronouns that are frequently misspelled. The last eight are common pairs of homophones. Dozens of additional homophone sets could have been selected for this activity, but the ones selected are those that are most frequently misused. Note also that there are two sets of these items that would need to be used in groups of three rather than in pairs. These are **their, there, they're** and **to, too, two.**

Avoiding Double Negatives: Six pop-up cards are provided for this usage skill. These are **any, ever, never, nobody,** and **anybody**—plus Usage Pop-Up Card 61, **no,** (to serve as one in the pair with **any**). (These are Usage Pop-Up Cards 66-70.) In most cases students would deal with these in pairs, such as **any** and **no.** Instructional wording for this level may vary, but here is one possibility: "You have two cards on your desk. One has the word **any** and the other **no.** I am going to show you a sentence that has a blank space. If the word **any** would fit into that space, please hold up that card. If the word **no** fits, please hold up that card. The first sentence is *I don't have _____ money.* Hold up one of your cards. (Allow time for answers.) That's right, the answer is **any.** *I don't have **any** money.* The next sentence is . . ." Proceed likewise with your choices of other word pairs for this skill. Note that there are many additional words that may be chosen as pairs for helping students avoid double negatives.

Correct Choices of Selected Adjectives and Adverbs: Eleven pop-up cards are provided for this usage skill. These are **good, well, better, best, bad, badly, worse, worst, much, more,** and **most.** (These are Usage Pop-Up Cards 71-81.) In most cases students would deal with these in pairs, such as **good** and **well.** Instructional wording for this concept may vary, but here is one possibility: "You have two cards on your desk. One has the word **good** and the other **well.** I am going to show you a sentence that has a blank space. If the word **good** would fit into that space, please hold up that card. If the word **well** fits, please hold up that card. The first sentence is *You danced very _____ in gym class today.* Hold up one of your cards. (Allow time for answers.) That's right, the answer is **well.** *You danced very **well** in gym class today.* The next sentence is . . ." Proceed likewise with your choices of other word pairs for this skill. Note that there are many different ways these cards may be grouped for usage instruction.

Starters for Correct Choices of Articles: (a or an)

DINOSAUR

ELEPHANT

Starters for Correct Choices of Singular or Plural Verbs: (is or are)

The men _____ driving the cars.

Everyone _____ hungry.

Starters for Correct Choices of Singular or Plural Verbs: (was or were)

One of the singers _____ loud.

The boys on the team _____ tall.

Starters for Correct Choices of Singular or Plural Verbs: (seems or seem)

The cats in the barn _____ lonely.

The dog _____ upset.

Starters for Correct Choices of Singular or Plural Verbs: (doesn't or don't)

It _____ matter.

Mary and Pam _____ want to go.

Dad says he _____ like ice cream.

Answers: a, an, are, is, was, were, seem, seems, doesn't, don't, doesn't

Starters for Correct Choices of Pronouns: (I or me)

My teacher and _____ will ride home together.

Give this to Ed and _____ later.

Sam and _____ sang a crazy song.

Starters for Correct Choices of Pronouns: (we or us)

_____, along with the coach, celebrated the win.

The money was for Tom and _____.

Starters for Correct Choices of Pronouns: (she or her—or he or him)

Paul and _____ swam until noon.

Give the report to Matt and _____ later.

Starters for Correct Choices of Pronouns: (they or them)

_____ helped with the chores.

This present is for Bob and _____.

Starters for Correct Choices of Pronouns: (who or whom)

George, _____ is now sad, really wanted to win.

I wrote, "To _____ it may concern."

Answers: I, me, I, We, us, she/he, her/him, They, them, who, whom

Starters for Correct Choices of Verb Tenses: (saw or seen)

No one _____ Jimmy leave the room.

They have never _____ such beauty.

I have just _____ a terrific movie.

Starters for Correct Choices of Verb Tenses: (ran or run)

I _____ home fast.

Have you ever _____ in the race?

Starters for Correct Choices of Verb Tenses: (did or done)

I _____ my chores quickly.

I have never _____ them so fast.

Starters for Correct Choices of Verb Tenses: (went or gone)

We _____ to an early movie.

I've always _____ home late.

Starters for Correct Choices of Verb Tenses: (began or begun)

The show _____ on time.

Had it _____ before we left?

Answers: saw, seen, seen, ran, run, did, done, went, gone, began, begun

Starters for Correct Choices of Verb Tenses: (knew or known)

He _____ the answer.

Have you ever _____ about this?

Starters for Correct Choices of Verb Tenses: (rode or ridden)

Tony _____ the horse.

He has _____ it quite often.

Starters for Correct Choices of Frequently Misused Verbs: (can or may)

I want to know if you _____ lift this box.

_____ I have an extra piece of pie?

Starters for Correct Choices of Frequently Misused Verbs: (set or sit)

Will you _____ down while we talk?

_____ the package on the table.

Starters for Correct Choices of Frequently Misused Verbs: (sat or set)

We _____ there for a very long time.

We _____ the plants on the window sill.

That was the longest I have ever _____ at once.

Answers: knew, known, rode, ridden, can, May, sit, Set, sat, set, sat

Starters for Correct Choices of Frequently Misused Verbs: (lay or laid)

Ed _____ the box down.

I was late because I _____ in bed too long.

Starters for Correct Choices of Frequently Misused Verbs: (lain or laid)

Dad has _____ on the couch for two hours.

They have _____ the matter to rest.

Starters for Correct Choices of Frequently Misused Verbs: (teach or learn)

I will soon _____ how to cook.

_____ me my multiplication tables.

Starters for Appropriate Spellings of Homophones and Possessives: (its and it's)

Tell me when _____ time to go.

Every dog has _____ day.

Starters for Appropriate Spellings of Homophones and Possessives: (their, there, or they're)

The money is never _____ when we need it.

_____ here!

_____ car is new.

Answers: laid, lay, lain, laid, learn, Teach, it's, its, there, They're, Their

GA1497

Starters for Appropriate Spellings of Homophones and Possessives: (your or you're)

Is this _____ paper?

_____ the winner!

Starters for Appropriate Spellings of Homophones and Possessives: (who's or whose)

_____ been in my room?

_____ dirty dishes are these?

Starters for Appropriate Spellings of Homophones and Possessives: (to, too or two)

There were only _____ bites left.

_____ work we go!

Kevin wants to go _____.

Starters for Appropriate Spellings of Homophones and Possessives: (no or know)

I don't _____ what to do next.

We want _____ more trouble.

Starters for Appropriate Spellings of Homophones and Possessives: (new or knew)

I have a _____ bicycle.

We _____ about the program.

Answers: your, You're, Who's, Whose, two, To, too, know, no, new, knew

Starters for Appropriate Spellings of Homophones and Possessives: (here or hear)

Can you _____ me?

Leave the plates _____ on the table.

Starters for Avoiding Double Negatives: (any or no—pull Usage Card #61)

There aren't _____ potato chips left.

We want _____ trouble.

Starters for Avoiding Double Negatives: (ever or never)

She doesn't _____ cry.

I've _____ seen you ride your bike.

Starters for Avoiding Double Negatives: (nobody or anybody)

Mom never lets _____ have an extra dessert.

_____ remained at school.

Starters for Correct Choices of Selected Adjectives or Adverbs: (good or well)

I am a _____ student.

She sang very _____ today.

You did a _____ job on your assignment.

Answers: hear, here, any, no, ever, never, anybody, Nobody, good, well, good

GA1497

Starters for Correct Choices of Selected Adjectives or Adverbs: (better or best)

Kay was the _____ leader in the whole school.

Of the two given, Max gave the _____ answer.

Starters for Correct Choices of Selected Adjectives or Adverbs: (bad or badly)

I felt _____ about my job.

That was a _____ thing to do.

Don't feel _____ over the weather.

Starters for Correct Choices of Selected Adjectives or Adverbs: (worse or worst)

This was the _____ storm in history.

It was even _____ than the last one.

Of Hugo and Diane, Hugo was the _____.

Starters for Correct Choices of Selected Adjectives or Adverbs: (much, more, or most)

We've never had _____ rain before now.

This story was the _____ frightening of all.

Of the two movies, this was the _____ popular.

Answers: best, better, bad, bad, bad, worst, worse, worse, much, most, more

GA1497

Cards for Usage Pop-Up
See page 10 for preparation instructions.

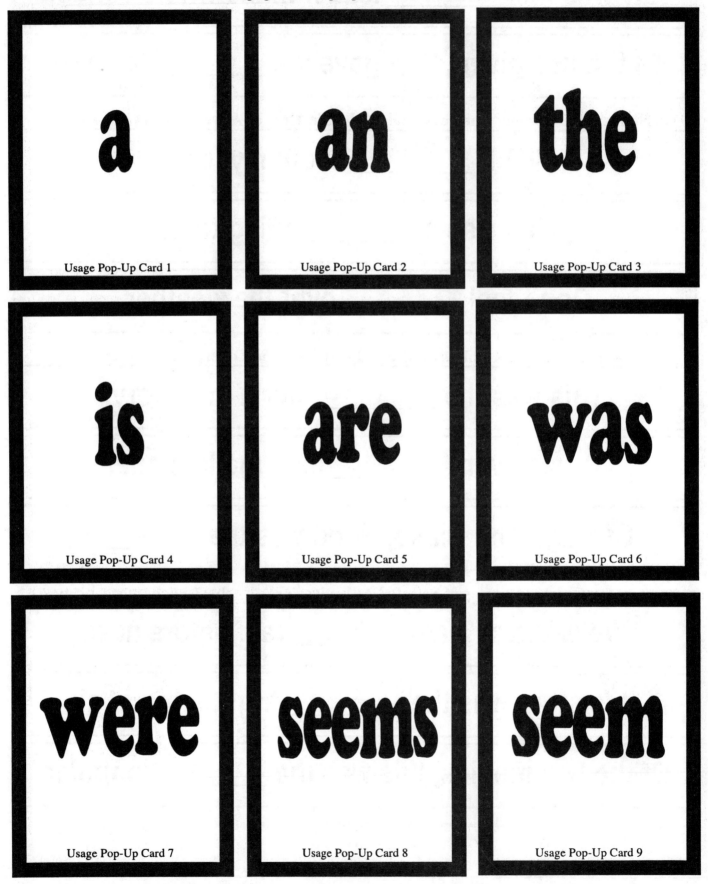

a

Usage Pop-Up Card 1

an

Usage Pop-Up Card 2

the

Usage Pop-Up Card 3

is

Usage Pop-Up Card 4

are

Usage Pop-Up Card 5

was

Usage Pop-Up Card 6

were

Usage Pop-Up Card 7

seems

Usage Pop-Up Card 8

seem

Usage Pop-Up Card 9

GA1497

Cards for Usage Pop-Up (Continued)
See page 10 for preparation instructions.

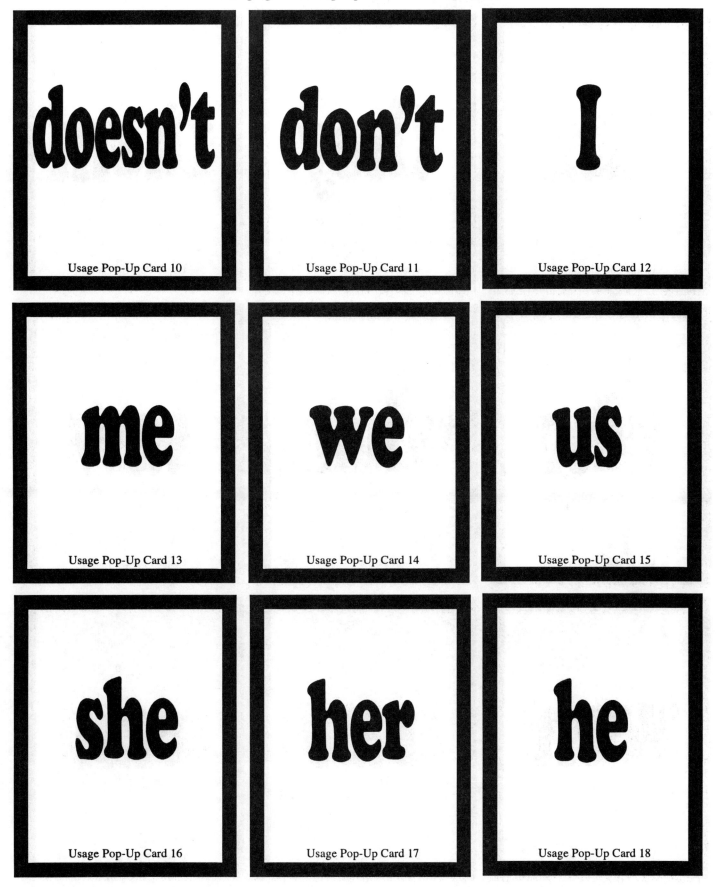

doesn't

Usage Pop-Up Card 10

don't

Usage Pop-Up Card 11

I

Usage Pop-Up Card 12

me

Usage Pop-Up Card 13

we

Usage Pop-Up Card 14

us

Usage Pop-Up Card 15

she

Usage Pop-Up Card 16

her

Usage Pop-Up Card 17

he

Usage Pop-Up Card 18

GA1497

him

Usage Pop-Up Card 19

they

Usage Pop-Up Card 20

them

Usage Pop-Up Card 21

who

Usage Pop-Up Card 22

whom

Usage Pop-Up Card 23

saw

Usage Pop-Up Card 24

seen

Usage Pop-Up Card 25

ran

Usage Pop-Up Card 26

run

Usage Pop-Up Card 27

GA1497

Cards for Usage Pop-Up (Continued)
See page 10 for preparation instructions.

did

Usage Pop-Up Card 28

done

Usage Pop-Up Card 29

went

Usage Pop-Up Card 30

gone

Usage Pop-Up Card 31

began

Usage Pop-Up Card 32

begun

Usage Pop-Up Card 33

knew

Usage Pop-Up Card 34

known

Usage Pop-Up Card 35

rode

Usage Pop-Up Card 36

GA1497

See page 10 for preparation instructions.

ridden

Usage Pop-Up Card 37

can

Usage Pop-Up Card 38

may

Usage Pop-Up Card 39

set

Usage Pop-Up Card 40

sit

Usage Pop-Up Card 41

sat

Usage Pop-Up Card 42

lie

Usage Pop-Up Card 43

lay

Usage Pop-Up Card 44

lain

Usage Pop-Up Card 45

GA1497

See page 10 for preparation instructions.

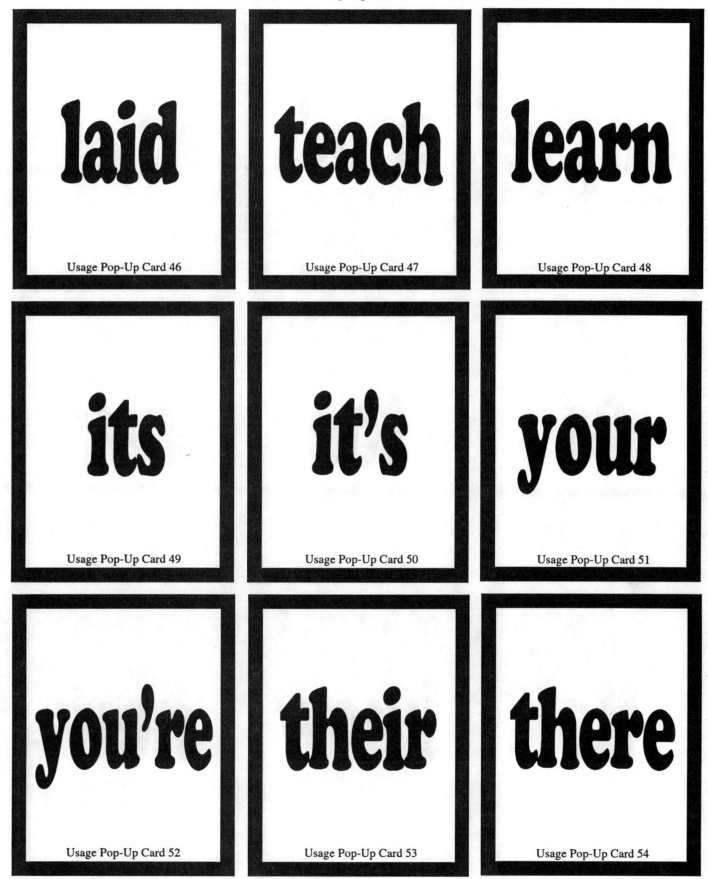

laid

Usage Pop-Up Card 46

teach

Usage Pop-Up Card 47

learn

Usage Pop-Up Card 48

its

Usage Pop-Up Card 49

it's

Usage Pop-Up Card 50

your

Usage Pop-Up Card 51

you're

Usage Pop-Up Card 52

their

Usage Pop-Up Card 53

there

Usage Pop-Up Card 54

GA1497

Cards for Usage Pop-Up (Continued)
See page 10 for preparation instructions.

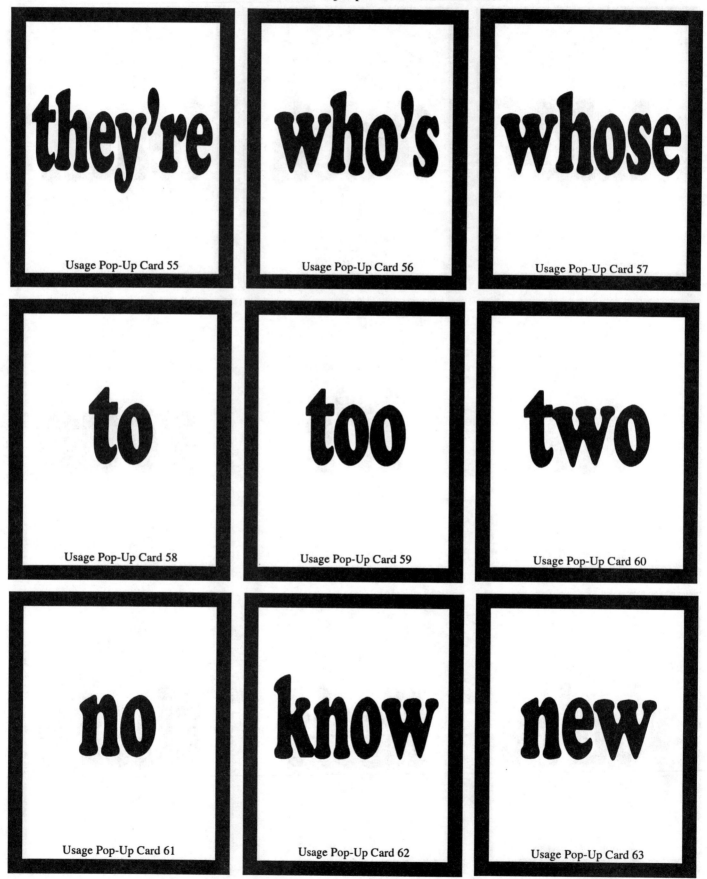

they're

Usage Pop-Up Card 55

who's

Usage Pop-Up Card 56

whose

Usage Pop-Up Card 57

to

Usage Pop-Up Card 58

too

Usage Pop-Up Card 59

two

Usage Pop-Up Card 60

no

Usage Pop-Up Card 61

know

Usage Pop-Up Card 62

new

Usage Pop-Up Card 63

GA1497

See page 10 for preparation instructions.

here	**hear**	**any**
Usage Pop-Up Card 64	Usage Pop-Up Card 65	Usage Pop-Up Card 66
ever	**never**	**nobody**
Usage Pop-Up Card 67	Usage Pop-Up Card 68	Usage Pop-Up Card 69
anybody	**good**	**well**
Usage Pop-Up Card 70	Usage Pop-Up Card 71	Usage Pop-Up Card 72

GA1497

Cards for Usage Pop-Up (Continued)
See page 10 for preparation instructions.

better

Usage Pop-Up Card 73

best

Usage Pop-Up Card 74

bad

Usage Pop-Up Card 75

badly

Usage Pop-Up Card 76

worse

Usage Pop-Up Card 77

worst

Usage Pop-Up Card 78

much

Usage Pop-Up Card 79

more

Usage Pop-Up Card 80

most

Usage Pop-Up Card 81

GA1497

An Overview of Language Mechanics for TEACHERS

GA1497

Teachers, as users and modelers of language, need a periodic review of the intricacies of language mechanics—not only to model more accurately for younger learners, but also to improve their own written and spoken communication skills.

My most frequently heard request from teachers regarding the topic of language mechanics has been, "Give us a *brief* set of guidelines for us to use as adult thinkers." Here is an overview.

GA1497

An Overview of Language Mechanics for TEACHERS

A serious teacher who wishes to create students who are accurate language users must engage in one activity at all times: *model accurate language.* The principles of speaking and writing must be learned, practiced, and *demonstrated* for students. These principles will extend far beyond those covered by the language arts text for the specific grade level being taught.

Our English language is complex. It does, however, conform to a system of logical patterning both in its printed and spoken forms. The majority of Americans never fully understand the mechanics of the printed system, although most manage to communicate their thoughts satisfactorily. Those who desire to grasp the complexities of the language, particularly the mechanics of formally recording the printed word, can gradually master the process via serious study and thought. There are many guides and manuals of style to assist the learner in this process. Some of these guides describe language from a "modern" point of view, and others view it more traditionally. The overview presented here intentionally does not include every imaginable rule with its many exceptions, but instead it provides teachers with a simplistic coverage of the language structure that might answer the majority of their questions. At times a more detailed manual will be required for answers to very unusual cases. Note that the information in these sources will vary from one manual to another. Comma rules, for instance, may have many different descriptions regarding their placement and use. This overview reflects the more recent views whenever manuals have differed.

Simplistic, condensed, and precise wording is used throughout this overview of English language mechanics, beginning with a look at the **sentence** and its components. Next is an examination of the eight **parts of speech**—a traditional concept without which the complete process cannot easily be understood. After these terms have been presented, then **usage** concepts are explained, followed by basic **punctuation** and **capitalization** generalizations.

SENTENCE INFORMATION

THE SENTENCE

A sentence is a group of words having a subject and predicate and expressing a complete thought.

PARTS OF A SENTENCE

Subject

The subject of a sentence is the doer of the action (exceptions involve the passive voice). It names the person, place, or thing being talked about.

Simple Subject
The simple subject is the specific word or words indicating who/what is doing the action or being talked about.
- **Birds** fly.
- A very tall **man** peered through the window.
- On First Street is that very elegant and beautiful **building**.

Complete Subject
The complete subject includes the simple subject with all its descriptors.
- **A very tall man** peered through the window.
- On First Street is **that very elegant and beautiful building**.

Compound Subject
A compound subject consists of two or more words generally joined by *and* or *or.*
- Either my **mother** or my **father** will eat the cake.
- The **teacher**, her **students**, and the **principal** went to the zoo.

Predicate
The predicate is the part that says something about the subject. It tells the action of the sentence or the state of being.

Simple Predicate
The simple predicate is the specific word or words that express the action. It is always a verb.
- Birds **fly**.
- A very tall man **peered** through the window.
- On First Street **is** that very elegant and beautiful building.

Complete Predicate
The complete predicate is the simple predicate with all its modifiers.
- A very tall man **peered through the window**.
- **On First Street is** that very elegant and beautiful building.

Compound Predicate
The compound predicate consists of two or more verbs generally joined by *and* or *or.*
- The player **ran** down the court and **scored** two points.
- I **will call** you or **come** to your house before noon.

Predicate Complement
The complement is a word or words that complete the meaning or action of the predicate. Object complements may be direct objects or indirect objects. Subject complements may be predicate nominatives or predicate adjectives. Each of these is explained separately in the section on parts of speech.

TYPES OF SENTENCES

Declarative Sentence
A declarative sentence makes a statement. It always ends with a period.
- Birds sing.

Interrogative Sentence
An interrogative sentence asks a question. It always ends with a question mark.
- Can birds sing?

Imperative Sentence
An imperative sentence makes a request or gives a command. The subject is usually understood to be the pronoun "you," although the word *you* does not appear in the sentence.
- Bring the packages to the picnic.

Exclamatory Sentence
An exclamatory sentence expresses strong feeling. It always ends with an exclamation mark.
- Don't let him sing!

GA1497

SENTENCE FORMS

Simple Sentence
A simple sentence has only one main clause and no dependent clause.
- Birds sing.

Compound Sentence
A compound sentence has two or more main clauses but no dependent clauses.
- Birds sing and cows moo.
- Paul ran but Mary walked.
- The president of the large company left the meeting, but no one followed him.

Complex Sentence
A complex sentence has one main clause and one or more dependent clauses.
- Sally is happy because she is in good health.
- I want what is best for everyone.
- Paul ran while Mary walked.
- The tiny puppy and its owner marched through the streets before the stores opened for business.
- The man who dressed in black introduced the star before she arrived.
- After the meal was finished, the president of the large company left the meeting.

Compound-Complex Sentence
A compound-complex sentence contains two or more main clauses and one or more dependent clauses.
- Before Ann spoke, I laughed and Mary cried.
- After the meal was finished, the president of the large company left the meeting, but no one followed him.

SENTENCE ERRORS

Sentence Fragment
A sentence fragment is a group of words that does not express a complete thought. Although it is not a complete sentence, the fragment is often written with a capital letter and with end punctuation.
- Oh, those teen-agers! (No verb)
- Just pretending to be asleep. (No subject or verb)

Run-On Sentence
A run-on sentence consists of two or more main clauses that are run together without proper punctuation as if they were one sentence. These are unacceptable in formal writing.
- The thunder clapped loudly the lightning was bright.
- I saw the man, I wanted to scream.
- Sally fed the baby, it had cried for hours.

THE PHRASE

A phrase is a group of related words that do not express a complete thought and do not have both a subject and predicate. There are **noun phrases** (such as the complete subject) and **verb phrases** (such as the complete predicate).

PREPOSITIONAL PHRASE

A prepositional phrase starts with a preposition and is followed by one or more related words.
- They fell from the top of the building.
- In the morning I go to the store on the corner.

These prepositional phrases are used as either adjectives or adverbs.

Adjectival/Prepositional Phrase
This type of phrase describes a noun or a pronoun.
- That boy in my class is a good student.
- I chose the one without a problem.

Adverbial/Prepositional Phrase
This type of phrase modifies a verb, an adjective, or an adverb. The phrase generally tells **how, when, where,** or **why**.
- Mary went to school.
- My dress is red with white polka dots.
- They met late in the afternoon.

VERBAL PHRASE

Participial Phrase
A participle is an -*ing* form of a verb that is used as an adjective. A participial phrase begins with a participle and is followed by its modifiers and complement. The phrase is used as an adjective.
- Everyone saw Mary **drinking her milk**.
- **Running very fast**, I tried to win the race.

Gerund Phrase
A gerund is an -*ing* form of a verb that is used as a noun.
- **Playing** is fun. (*Playing* is the gerund and is also the subject of the sentence.)

A gerund phrase begins with the gerund and is followed by its modifiers and complement. The complete phrase is used as a noun.
- **Playing basketball** is fun. (This phrase is the subject of the sentence. *Playing* is the gerund.)
- I like **watching movies**. (This phrase is the direct object. *Watching* is the gerund.)
- Jerry was punished for **hitting the dog**. (The phrase is the object of the preposition *for. Hitting* is the gerund.)

Infinitive Phrase
An infinitive is a verb form using the word *to* (such as *to run, to see*, or *to be*). A complete infinitive phrase includes the infinitive, its modifiers, and a possible complement. The phrase may be used as a noun, an adjective, or an adverb. Note that there is a difference in the word *to* used as part of an infinitive phrase and the word *to* used in a prepositional phrase.
- **To win** was his goal. (The infinitive phrase is used as a noun as the subject of the sentence.)
- He ran **to win**. (The infinitive phrase is used as an adverb modifying the verb *ran*.)
- The man **to see** goes to my school. (The infinitive phrase is used as an adjective indicating which man. Note that the phrase *to my school* is a prepositional phrase.)

THE CLAUSE

A clause is a group of words with a subject and a predicate.

MAIN (INDEPENDENT) CLAUSE
A main clause is a group of words that can stand alone as a simple sentence.
- **Mary spoke**.
- **Mary spoke** to the man.
- **Mary spoke** when she wanted to.

DEPENDENT CLAUSE
A dependent clause is a group of words with a subject and predicate, but one that *depends* on the remainder of the sentence for its meaning. A dependent clause does not express a complete thought and cannot stand alone. It must always be attached to a main clause as a part of a sentence. These clauses may be used as nouns, adjectives, or adverbs.
- I know **that you hid the book**. (This noun clause is used as a direct object.)
- Your gift will be **whatever you want**. (This noun clause is used as the predicate nominative.)
- **What I do** should not matter to him. (This noun clause is used as the subject of the sentence.)
- The one **who gives me a dollar** will receive the prize. (This adjective clause tells which one. It modifies the pronoun *one*.)

GA1497

- We studied about animals **that sleep during the winter.** (This adjective clause tells what kind.)
- **When I finish my chores,** I will go with you. (This clause is used as an adverb telling when.)
- Sam found his papers **where he had left them.** (This clause is used as an adverb telling where.)

PARTS OF SPEECH

NOUN

A noun is a word used to name a person, place, thing, or idea. A word must be used in a sentence before the part of speech is clear. For example, the word *play* may be used as a verb (Jerry will play ball) or as a noun (Here are tickets for the play).

KINDS OF NOUNS

Proper Noun
A proper noun is a word that names a specific person, place, or thing. Proper nouns are always capitalized. *(Sally, Abraham Lincoln, Tennessee, Mississippi River, Washington Elementary School, New Orleans)*

Common Noun
A common noun names a category of a person, place, or thing without being specific. The following are four types of common nouns.

Collective Noun
A collective noun names a group or collection. *(flock, class, army, choir, team)*

Concrete Noun
A concrete noun names something material in form. This is usually something that can be touched. *(bush, chair, car)*

Abstract Noun
An abstract noun names a quality or idea. It can generally not be touched. *(freedom, love, friendliness, apathy)*

Compound Noun
A compound noun is made up of two or more words. It can be written as one word, as a hyphenated word, or as two words. *(blackberry, father-in-law, high school)*

PRONOUN

A pronoun is a word that takes the place of a noun. A pronoun is not to be confused with a common noun such as *boy*. The word *boy* might take the place of *Jerry Jones*, but a **pronoun** such as *he* can replace either.

KINDS OF PRONOUNS

Personal Pronoun
A personal pronoun tells who is speaking, spoken to, or spoken of.

Chart of Personal Pronouns
Showing Case, Person, and Number

SINGULAR

	Nominative Case	Possessive Case	Objective Case
1st person	I	my mine	me
2nd person	you	your yours	you
3rd person	he	his	him
	she	her hers	her

PLURAL

1st person	we	our ours	us
2nd person	you	your yours	you
3rd person	they	their theirs	them

Interrogative Pronoun
An interrogative pronoun is one that asks a question. They are *who, whose, whom, which,* and *what.*
- **Who** is coming for dinner?
- **Which** is yours?

Note that *who, whose, whom, which,* and *what* can also be used as relative pronouns.

Relative Pronoun
A relative pronoun generally begins a dependent clause and relates that clause to the rest of the sentence. The relative pronouns are *who, whose, whom, which,* and *that.*
- I know the man **who** is coming for dinner.
- Tell your teacher **which** book belongs to you.
- The dessert **that** I like most is chocolate cake.

Indefinite Pronoun
An indefinite pronoun gives a general or nonspecific (indefinite) impression. Examples are *any, anybody, anyone, anything, all, everybody, either, enough, nobody, no one, none, nothing, both, several, more, most, few, many, less, little, another, one, some, everyone, somebody, each,* etc.
- **Everybody** on the team was happy.
- **No one** asked for **anything** from **anyone.**
- **Few** refused **both** the coins.

Note that some of these words are also used as adjectives, depending upon the sentence construction. In the sentences *Both boys refused the money* and *There were few people in attendance*, the words *both* and *few* are adjectives instead of pronouns.

Reflexive Pronoun
A reflexive pronoun compounds a personal pronoun with *-self* or *-selves.* Sometimes a reflexive pronoun is called an intensive pronoun.
- He hurt **himself** during the game.
- They gave **themselves** a superior rating.

Note that in formal writing, words like *hisself, themself,* and *theirselves* should not be used.

Demonstrative Pronoun
A demonstrative pronoun points out something definite. *(this, that, these, those)*
- **This** is a great book to read.
- **Those** were the good old days!

Note that these same words may also be used as adjectives in sentences such as *This book is great* or *Those days were good.*

USES OF NOUNS OR PRONOUNS

Subject of a Verb
See the earlier explanation of simple, complete, and compound subjects in the sentence section.
- **Ed** left the room.
- **We** attended the play.

Direct Object
The direct object is a noun or pronoun that receives the action of the verb or shows the result of the action. It answers the question *what* or *whom* after an action verb.
- Jerry sliced the **orange.** (Noun as direct object)
- No one helped **me** with the lesson. (Pronoun as direct object)

Indirect Object
The indirect object is a noun or pronoun that goes before the direct object and generally tells **to whom** or **for whom** the action of the verb is done—without using the word *to.* There cannot be an indirect object without a direct object. Indirect objects usually follow verbs such as *gave, brought, took, offered, showed,* etc.

GA1497

- Ed gave **Lee** a present. (Note that if this sentence read *Ed gave a present to Lee*, there would be no indirect object.)
- John offered **him** a job. (Pronoun as indirect object)
- My mother saved **me** the pie. (Pronoun as indirect object)

Object of a Preposition
A noun or pronoun can be used as the object of a preposition.
- Kevin looked through the **telescope**. (Noun as object of the preposition)
- Bob talked to **me**. (Pronoun as object of the preposition)

Subject Complement (Predicate Nominative)
A predicate nominative is a noun or pronoun that follows a linking verb and refers to the subject. It is the same person or thing as the subject and can usually be interchanged with it. (A subject complement can also be an adjective.)
- Mark is the **leader**. (The word *leader* refers to *Mark*, and the two words are interchangeable.)
- It was **he** who led the parade. (Note that errors are frequently made in formal grammar with the wrong case of the pronoun in the predicate nominative position. The word *him* would be incorrect in this sentence.)

Object of a Verbal
A noun or pronoun can be used as the object of verbals. The three verbals are gerunds, participles, and infinitives. See an earlier section for an explanation of these verbals.
- Helping **him** was fun. (Pronoun as object of gerund *helping*)
- Ann observed Sally teaching **him**. (Pronoun as object of participle *teaching*)
- We like to see **Ed**. (Noun as object of infinitive *to see*)

Subject of Infinitive
A noun or pronoun can be the subject of verbals. Note that these words will be in the objective case.
- No one wanted **her** to see the movie. (Pronoun as subject of infinitive *to see*)

Appositive
An appositive is a noun or pronoun placed near another noun or pronoun to explain, restate, or identify its meaning.
- Ed, our **friend**, left the room. (Noun in apposition with *Ed*)
- This is George, my **brother**. (Noun in apposition with the predicate nominative *George*)

Direct Address
A noun or pronoun can be used to address someone directly. It is generally set off by commas. This usage is sometimes referred to as the nominative of direct address.
- **Ed**, our friend left the room. (Note that the only difference in this example and the appositive example above is the comma after *friend*. In this sentence Ed is directly addressed, but in the above sentence *Ed* is the subject.)

PLURALITY OF NOUNS OR PRONOUNS

Singular Number
A word is singular when it refers to one. (Nouns: *girl, ox*; pronouns: *this, myself, I, he, she, it*)

Plural Number
A word is plural when it denotes more than one. (Nouns: *girls, oxen*; pronouns: *these, ourselves, we, they, them*)

Person
1. First person refers to the speaker.
- **I** left **mine** at home.
- Leave **us** alone.

2. Second person refers to the one spoken to.
- **You** left **yours** at school.

3. Third person refers to the one spoken about.
- **He** left **his** at the ballpark.
- **They** left **theirs** at home.

GENDER OF NOUNS OR PRONOUNS
Gender denotes sex. The four genders are masculine, feminine, neuter, and common.

Masculine Gender
Masculine gender refers to the male sex. (Nouns: *boy, man*; pronouns: *he, him*)

Feminine Gender
Feminine gender refers to the female sex. (Nouns: *girl, woman*; pronouns: *she, her*)

Neuter Gender
Neuter gender refers to something without either sex. (Nouns: *tree, paper, door;* pronouns: *it, those*)

Common Gender
Common gender refers to either or both sexes. (Nouns: *children, pupil, teacher*; pronouns: *they, them*)

CASE OF NOUNS OR PRONOUNS

Nominative Case
Any noun can be in the nominative case; pronouns that can be used in the nominative case are *I, you, we, he, she, it, they,* and *who*.

The subject of a verb requires the nominative case.
- **I** am a positive person.
- Where are **they**?

A predicate nominative (subject complement) requires the nominative case. Note that informal English allows expressions such as *It's me* that violate this rule.
- The winners in our class are **Mark** and **I**.

A noun or pronoun used as an appositive requires the same case as the word it refers to.
- Your teachers, **Mr. Boyd** and **I**, will lead the parade. (Nominative case, in apposition with the subject)
- Apologies were made by two players, **Keith** and **me**. (Objective case, in apposition with the object of the preposition)

A noun or pronoun used as direct address will also be in the nominative case.
- **Bob**, take this note to Miss Ellis.
- Thank you, **Mrs. Jones**, for the great year at school.

Objective Case
A noun or pronoun used as a direct object, indirect object, object of a preposition, object of verbals, or subject of an infinitive will be in the objective case. Any noun can be in the objective case. Pronouns for the objective case are *me, us, you, him, her, it, them*, and *whom*. Frequent usage errors occur because of selecting the wrong case. Many of these errors occur in compound expressions. In such cases, listen to each word in the compound separately.
- Incorrect: **Him** and me went to town. (Would you say *Him went to town* or *Me went to town*?)
- Correct: **He** and I went to town. (Nominative case is needed because *He and I* is the subject of the sentence.)

The direct object requires the objective case.
- Mark found **him** at the zoo.
- Mark found **John** and **him** at the zoo.

The indirect object is in the objective case.
- Give **her** the pencil.
- Give **Sally** and **her** the pencil.

The object of a preposition requires the objective case.
- Incorrect: He shot at **Tom** and **I**. (Would it sound right to say *He shot at I*?)
- Correct: He shot at **Tom** and **me**. (Objective case is needed because *Tom and me* is the object of the preposition *for*.)
- Fred worked with **him**.
- Fred worked with **John** and **him**.

GA1497

The object of a gerund, participle, or infinitive will be in the objective case.
- Praising **him** is not the answer. (Object of gerund)
- To help **me** requires concentration. (Object of infinitive)
- The man calling **me** was deaf. (Object in participial phrase)

The subject of an infinitive requires the objective case.
- We wanted **her** to be our teacher.
- Fred wants **him** to fire me.

Possessive Case
The possessive case shows ownership. Most nouns may be made possessive by adding an apostrophe and *s*. Possessive pronouns are *my, mine, our, ours, his, her, hers, its, your, yours, their, theirs*, and *whose*. Some texts teach that *my* (as in *This is my book*) is a possessive <u>adjective</u> instead of a possessive pronoun. As long as the words are used correctly, either label is appropriate.
- This puzzle is **mine**.

The possessive case is used for pronouns preceding a gerund.
- **His** working late improved his scores.
- Ann approved of **their** including Lee.

VERB
A verb expresses physical or mental action or state of being.

KINDS OF VERBS

Regular Verb
Verbs are classified as either regular or irregular. A regular verb forms its past tense and past participle by adding *-ed, -d*, or *-t* to the present tense.

hear	heard	heard
walk	walked	walked
deal	dealt	dealt

Irregular Verb
An irregular verb forms its past tense and past participle by changing a vowel letter in the present tense or by other spelling changes.

begin	began	begun
go	went	gone
do	did	done

Transitive Verb
Verbs are either transitive or intransitive. A transitive verb needs an object to complete its meaning. This verb <u>transfers</u> the action from the doer to the receiver.
- We **ran** the race. (*Race* is the direct object.)
- I **spoke** harsh words. (*Words* is the direct object.)

Intransitive Verb
An intransitive verb expresses action without an object.
- We **ran** for a long time. (No object)
- I **spoke** softly. (No object)

Linking Verb
A linking verb is an intransitive verb that connects the subject to the predicate complement. They are sometimes called state-of-being verbs. Some common linking verbs are *be (am, is, are, was, were, been) seem, appear, feel, become, smell, taste,* and *sound.*
- Bill **seems** happy. (The linking verb *seems* connects the subject *Bill* with the predicate adjective *happy*.)
- Bill **is** our president. (The linking verb *is* connects the subject *Bill* with the predicate nominative *president*.)
- The lemon **turned** sour.
- The odor **grew** strong.

Note that verbs such as *turn* and *grow* may be either linking or transitive. Substitute the word *seem* to help you tell. *John grew tired* is an example of a linking verb. *John grew tomatoes*, however, is not.

Helping (Auxiliary) Verb
An auxiliary or helping verb helps to form the mood, voice, tense, etc., of other verbs. Examples are *be, am, is, are, was, were, been, do, may, has, have, shall*, and *will*.
- They **will have been** dancing for five hours. (The complete verb phrase is *will have been dancing*.)
- She **has** not **been** explaining this to you correctly.

PRINCIPAL PARTS OF VERBS
The principal parts of a verb are those from which its moods and tenses are formed. The principal parts are: present *(play, go, drink)*, past *(played, went, drank)*, and past participle *(played, gone, drunk)*.

VOICE OF VERBS
The voice of the verb refers to whether the subject of a sentence acts or is acted upon. A verb may be in the **active voice** or the **passive voice**.

Active Voice
A verb is in the active voice when the subject does the action.
- The crowd's cheers **encouraged** the team.
- The teacher **taught** the lesson.

Passive Voice
A verb is in the passive voice when the subject receives the action. Often the word *by* is a sign of the passive voice.
- The team **was inspired** by the crowd's cheers.
- The lesson **was taught** by the teacher.

TENSES OF VERBS
Tense indicates the time of the action.

Present Tense
Present tense indicates action that is going on at the present time. (John **studies**.)

Past Tense
Past tense indicates action completed at a specific time in the past. (John **studied** yesterday.)

Future Tense
Future tense indicates that action will take place in the future. The helping verb *will* (or in some cases *shall*) is always used with the future tense. The use of the word *shall* with the future tense is gradually becoming less frequent. (He **will study** soon.)

Present Perfect Tense
Present perfect tense indicates action completed at the present. The helping verbs *have* or *has* are always used with the present perfect tense. (John **has studied** in the past.)

Past Perfect Tense
Past perfect tense indicates an action completed before some indicated time in the past. The helping verb *had* is always used with the past perfect tense. (John **had studied** for the exam.)

Future Perfect Tense
Future perfect tense indicates that action will be completed before a certain time in the future. This tense is used relatively infrequently. The helping verbs *will have* (or in some cases *shall have*) are always used with the future perfect tense. The use of the word *shall* with the future perfect tense is gradually becoming less frequent. (John **will have studied** for the exam before he takes it.)

MOODS OF VERBS

Indicative Mood
A verb in the indicative mood states a fact or asks a question. Most sentences are in the indicative mood.
- George **won** the grand prize.
- **Are** you **feeling** well?

GA1497

Imperative Mood

A verb in the imperative mood expresses a command or makes a request. *You* is the subject of the sentence in the imperative mood, but it is not stated or written.
- **Leave** this house immediately.
- **Paint** the shelf.

Subjunctive Mood

The subjunctive mood is used relatively rarely in modern speech and writing. A verb in the subjunctive mood expresses a doubt, a condition contrary to fact, a wish or regret, or a supposition. The clause in the subjunctive mood is usually introduced by *if*. The other clause is usually in the indicative mood.
- If I **were** (subjunctive) ill, I'd call you (indicative).

CONJUGATION OF VERBS

A conjugation shows the arrangement or chart of the voices, moods (limited below to the indicative), tenses, persons, and number of the verb.

CONJUGATION OF THE VERB *TO SEE*
Indicative Mood
ACTIVE VOICE

Singular	Plural
Present Tense	
1. I see	we see
2. you see	you see
3. he (she, it) sees	they see
Past Tense	
1. I saw	we saw
2. you saw	you saw
3. he (she, it) saw	they saw
Future Tense	
1. I will (shall) see	we will (shall) see
2. you will see	you will see
3. he (she, it) will see	they will see
Present Perfect Tense	
1. I have seen	we have seen
2. you have seen	you have seen
3. he has seen	they have seen
Past Perfect Tense	
1. I had seen	we had seen
2. you had seen	you had seen
3. he (she, it) had seen	they had seen
Future Perfect Tense	
1. I will (shall) have seen	we will (shall) have seen
2. you will have seen	you will have seen
3. he (she, it) will have seen	they will have seen

Indicative Mood
Passive Voice

Singular	Plural
Present Tense	
1. I am seen	we are seen
2. you are seen	you are seen
3. he (she, it) is seen	they are seen
Past Tense	
1. I was seen	we were seen
2. you were seen	you were seen
3. he (she, it) was seen	they were seen
Future Tense	
1. I shall be seen	we shall be seen
2. you will be seen	you will be seen
3. he (she, it) will be seen	they will be seen
Present Perfect Tense	
1. I have been seen	we have been seen
2. you have been seen	you have been seen
3. he (she, it) has been seen	they have been seen
Past Perfect Tense	
1. I had been seen	we had been seen
2. you had been seen	you had been seen
3. he (she, it) had been seen	they had been seen
Future Perfect Tense	
1. I shall have been seen	we shall have been seen
2. you will have been seen	you will have been seen
3. he (she, it) will have been seen	they will have been seen

ADJECTIVE

An adjective describes a noun or pronoun. It usually answers what kind, how many, or which one.
- **Three** people remained. (*Three* describes the noun *people*.)
- The **tall** one is my father. (*Tall* describes the pronoun *one*.)
- The ad was **dull**. (*Dull* is a predicate adjective describing *ad*.)

Articles

The adjectives *a, an,* and *the* are sometimes called articles. Articles are definite (*the*) or indefinite (*a* or *an*).

Comparison of Adjectives

Adjectives may be compared by degrees: positive, comparative, and superlative.

Positive	Comparative	Superlative
good	better	best
bad	worse	worst
far (distance)	farther	farthest
many (much)	more	most
beautiful	more beautiful	most beautiful

Note that the comparative degree is always used when only two people or items are being compared. The superlative degree is used when three or more are being compared.
- Bob is a **better** student than George.
- Bob is the **best** student in the entire class.
- Sally is the **taller** captain of the two teams.
- Sally is the **tallest** player on the team.

Be sure not to use an incorrect double form of an adjective such as *more beautifuler* or *most farthest*.

Predicate Adjective

A predicate adjective follows a linking verb and describes the subject of the sentence.
- Mary was so **happy**.
- Tomorrow will be **cold** and **damp**.

ADVERB

An adverb is a word that modifies a verb, an adjective, or another adverb. An adverb modifying a verb tells **how, when, where,** and **to what extent,** and many end with -*ly*.
- He walked **quietly**. (Tells how)
- He walked **frequently**. (Tells when)
- He walked **there**. (Tells where)

Note that some words ending in -*ly* are not adverbs. In the sentences *He has a stately office* and *The dog is friendly*, the words *stately* and *friendly* are both adjectives.

Comparison of Adverbs

Adverbs, like adjectives, have positive, comparative, and superlative degrees.

Positive	Comparative	Superlative
well	better	best
badly	worse	worst
happily	more happily	most happily
far (extent)	further	furthest

Sometimes adjectives (such as *round, square, dead*) and some adverbs (*uniquely*) cannot be compared.

PREPOSITION

A preposition is a word that helps show how a noun or pronoun relates to another part of the sentence. Some common prepositions are *to, at, in, on, up, by, for, from, with, under, over, above, between, after, out, behind, into,* and *around*. Some two-word prepositions are *along with, apart from, as for, due to, out of, up to, because of* and *except for*. Some three-word prepositions are *on account of, by means of, by way of, in case of, in place of,* and *in front of*.
- **Because of** the rain, the play was moved **to** the auditorium.

GA1497

CONJUNCTION

A conjunction connects words or groups of words.

Coordinate Conjunctions
Coordinate conjunctions connect words, phrases, and clauses of equal rank. Some common coordinate conjunctions are *and, or, but, nor, for, so*, and *yet*.
- Bill **and** Mary washed **and** dried the dishes.
- Bill washed the dishes, **but** Mary dried them.

Correlative Conjunctions
Correlative conjunctions occur in pairs and also connect words, phrases, and clauses of equal rank. Some common correlative conjunctions are *both/and, either/or, not only/but also, neither/nor*, and *whether/or*.
- **Both** Bill **and** Mary washed the dishes.
- **Either** Bill **or** Mary washed the dishes.

Subordinate Conjunctions
Subordinate conjunctions connect subordinate (dependent) clauses to main clauses. Some common subordinate conjunctions are *if, after, although, as, as if, as much as, as long as, as soon as, as though, because, before, if, since, so that, than, though, unless, until, when, whenever, where, wherever, whether*, and *while*.
- The dog will follow you **if** you feed it.
- **While** you are young, you should learn a foreign language.

Note that many of these words may also be used as other parts of speech. In the sentences *I left before noon* and *Where are you going*, the words *before* and *where* are used as adverbs instead of conjunctions.

INTERJECTION

Interjections express strong feeling. They are independent of the sentence and are not used very often. Examples are *Boo! Wow! Sh-h-h! Oh! Ah! Hey! Ouch! Help!* Some are followed by commas and some by an exclamation mark, depending upon the degree of emphasis.
- **Well,** I see you're home.
- **Well!** I'm shocked!
- **Ah,** this is a peaceful scene.
- **Ah!** I've caught you now!

USAGE

AGREEMENT OF SUBJECT AND PREDICATE

A singular subject should always have a singular predicate, and a plural subject should always have a plural predicate.
- The **cat is** brown. (singular)
- Those **cats are** brown. (plural)

Words between the subject and the predicate do not affect the plurality of the subject and the predicate. Prepositional phrases and expressions such as *accompanied by, together with, as well as, including*, etc., do not affect the number of the subject. These phrases, however, often cause usage errors.
- The **cat is** brown.
- The **cat** belonging to those boys **is** brown.
- Those **cats are** brown.
- Those **cats**, as well as this dog, **are** brown.

Compound subjects joined by *and* require a plural predicate.
- Bill and Mary **wash** the dishes.
- Basketball, football, and tennis **were** his hobbies.

When singular subjects are joined by *or* or *nor*, they require a singular predicate. If the first subject is singular and the second is plural, the predicate agrees with the nearer. The reverse is also true.
- Either Bill or Mary **is** our leader.
- Neither the team members nor Bill **was** happy with the loss.
- Either Bill or the twins **were** next.

The indefinite pronouns *each, either, neither, someone, somebody, something, anyone, anybody, anything, everyone, everybody, everything, little, much, no one, nobody, nothing, other, one*, and *another* take singular predicates.
- Each **was** included on the honor roll.
- Each of the students **was** included on the honor roll.
- Neither **was** present for the roll call.
- Neither of the players **was** present for the roll call.

The indefinite pronouns *both, few, many, others*, and *several* take plural predicates.
- Both **were** winners.
- Several **shine** in the dark.

The indefinite pronouns *all, any, more, most, none, some*, and *enough* may have either singular or plural predicates. Go by what sounds best in the sentence.
- All of the money **was** spent.
- All of the boys **were** tall.
- None of the cake **was** eaten.
- None of the men **were** awake.

Collective nouns have singular predicates if the group is regarded as a unit. They have plural predicates if the parts of the unit are viewed as separate units.
- The couple **is** going to party. (Unit)
- The couple **were** discussing me. (Separate units)
- The team **was** winning the game. (Unit)
- The team **were** dividing the desserts. (Separate units)

Here, where, and *there* are never subjects. The predicate will agree with its (following) subject.
- Where **is** my book?
- Where **are** my books?
- Here **is** the boy.
- Here **are** the boy and his father.

AGREEMENT OF PRONOUN AND ANTECEDENT

A pronoun should agree in number with its antecedent. An antecedent is the noun for which it stands.
- Mark found **his** ticket. (*Mark* is singular, and the possessive pronoun *his* is also singular.)
- The boys found **their** tickets. (Both *boys* and *their* are plural.)

Two or more singular antecedents joined by *and* need a plural pronoun.
- Kate and Joan have finished **their** meal.
- Both Tom and his father read **their** books.

Two or more singular antecedents joined by *or* or *nor* need a singular pronoun.
- Neither Kate nor Joan has finished **her** meal.
- Neither Tom nor his father read **his** book.

If one of two antecedents joined by *or* or *nor* is singular and one is plural, the pronoun agrees with the closer one.
- Neither Sally nor her classmates found **their** bus.
- Neither the classmates nor Sally found **her** bus.

Use a singular pronoun with antecedents as *one, each, either, neither, anyone, anybody, someone, somebody, everyone, everybody, kind, sort, no one*, and *nobody*.
- Everybody can open **her** Mother's Day gift.
- Everybody at both tables can show **her** Mother's Day gift.

Collective nouns may be singular or plural, depending upon how the unit is viewed.

GA1497

- The club is planning **its** dinner. (Singular)
- The couple are planning **their** responses. (Plural)

A pronoun should have the same *gender* as its antecedent.
- Joe ate **his** lunch. (Masculine)
- Mary wrote **her** name. (Feminine)
- The car was hit on **its** left side. (Neuter)
- Each player was given **his** or **her** ticket. (Common)

In some cases where the specific gender is not known, awkward phrasing may result. A sentence such as *Each player was given his or her ticket and told to find his or her bus before his or her parents left* can be reworded (when possible) to *Players were given their tickets and told to find their bus before their parents left.* It is considered incorrect to say *Each player was given their ticket . . .*

PRONOUNS FOLLOWING *THAN* OR *AS*

Be careful with pronouns that follow *than* or *as*. To choose the correct word, say the eliminated words.
- You are as hungry as **I**. (. . . as I am)
- Pam adores you more than **I**. (. . . more than I adore you)
- Pam adores you more than **me**. (. . . more than she adores me)

WHO AND WHOM

Who and *whoever* are in the nominative case, and *whom* and *whomever* are in the objective case. Use of the objective case has declined in informal language with these words.
- **Who** is your hero? (Subject)
- **Whom** is he calling? (Direct object)
- **Who** shall I say is calling? (Subject of *is calling*)
- To **whom** should I send this letter? (Object of a preposition)
- Al is a leader **whom** we all respect. (Object of verb *respect*)
- Al is a boy **who** we know will win. (Subject of *will win*)

WHO, WHICH, AND THAT

Who generally refers only to people. *Which* and *that* refer to animals or things. *That* may also refer to people.
- Give this to the teacher **that** directed the play. (Incorrect)
- Give this to the teacher **who** directed the play. (Corrected)
- I liked the rabbit **who** drank the milk. (Incorrect)
- I liked the rabbit **that** drank the milk. (Corrected)

When deciding whether to use *which* or *that*, a simple rule to follow is to use *that* in all cases when it sounds right.
- The money **which** I desperately need is gone. (Incorrect)
- The money **that** I desperately need is gone. (Corrected)

THEM, THESE, AND THOSE

The fact that *those* and *these* can be both pronouns and adjectives sometimes ultimately causes confusion with the use of the word *them*. *Them* is a pronoun only and cannot be used as an adjective.
- I have read **them** books. (Incorrect)
- I have read **those** books. (Corrected)
- I have read **these** books. (Corrected)

POINT OF VIEW

The same *person* of pronouns should be maintained in sentences and paragraphs. Do not shift from one class of person to another.
- **Those** hoping to swim should hurry, and **you** should arrive on time. (Incorrect shift from third person to second person)
- **Those** hoping to swim should hurry, and **we** should arrive on time. (Incorrect shift from third person to first person)
- **Those** hoping to swim should hurry, and **all** should arrive on time. (Correct—third person throughout)

Be cautious about unnecessary shifts in *number*.
- The **team** was excited over **its** win. **Their** victory was a

cause for celebration. (Incorrect—*it* and *their* both refer to the team, but *its* is singular and *their* is plural. A correct rephrasing might be either *their win* or *its victory*.)

Be cautious about unnecessary shifts in verb *tenses*.
- The wolf **ate** the grandmother, then he **waits** for Little Riding Hood. (Incorrect—shift from past to present tense. The word *waited* would correct the sentence.)

There are many reasons, however, for having different tenses in a passage.
- The author **reported** that Vitamin C **is** beneficial. (An example of an appropriate shift from past to present.)

Be cautious about unnecessary shifts in verb *voices*.
- Kendra **was liked** by her teacher, but the principal **resented** her. (Unnecessary shift from passive to active voice)
- Kendra **was liked** by her teacher but **was resented** by her principal. (Correct—passive only)

PARALLEL STRUCTURE

Parallel structure in writing should be maintained as carefully as possible. This should occur with words, phrases, and clauses.
- Ed is handsome, clever, smart, and has charm. (Lacks parallel word structure)
- Ed is handsome, clever, smart, and charming. (Corrected)
- The boy went through the forest, over the hill, and walked across the bridge. (Lacks parallel phrase structure)
- The boy went through the forest, over the hill, and across the bridge. (Corrected)
- I liked the pudding, Tina preferred the cake, Terri disliked the pie, and the tarts weren't wanted by anyone. (Lacks parallel clause structure)
- I liked the pudding, Tina preferred the cake, Terri favored the pie, and no one wanted the tarts. (Corrected)

Sometimes words need to be repeated for the best parallel construction.
- My friend and roommate left. (How many left?)
- Both my friend and my roommate left. (Better wording)

MODIFIERS AND DESCRIPTORS

Place adjective and adverb units near the words they describe. This positioning is very important in conveying the meaning.
- Todd wants only his money. (Nothing else)
- Only Todd wants his money. (No one else)
- Ed was informed after he won to mail in the form. (Not clear)
- After Ed won, he was informed to mail in the form. (Clearer)
- Ed was told to mail in the certificate after he won. (A very different meaning)
- Gnawing a hole in the roof, Jack saw the squirrel. (A dangling participial phrase)
- Jack saw the squirrel gnawing a hole in the roof. (Corrected)
- By practicing daily, the piece was soon learned. (A dangling gerund phrase)
- By practicing daily, Ned soon learned the piece. (Corrected)
- To make As, studying is a must. (Dangling infinitive phrase)
- To make good grades, one must study. (Corrected)

Use an adjective after a linking verb.

	is	
	appears	
	becomes	
The flower	*seems*	delicate. (not delicately)
	feels	
	looks	

Sometimes the linking verb *feel* is followed by an inappropriate adverb.
- I felt **badly** about that. (Incorrect)
- I felt **bad** about that. (Corrected)

AVOIDING DOUBLE NEGATIVES

A common usage error is the double negative. Although there are some reasons to have two negative words in one sentence, they are generally avoided. Words such as *hardly, scarcely, never, barely, not, -n't* (ending of some negative contractions), *nowhere, no, nothing, no one, nobody,* and *none* should generally occur only once per sentence.

- I **can't hardly** see. (Incorrect)
- I **can hardly** see. (Corrected)
- I **can't see** clearly. (Corrected)
- I **don't have no** money. (Incorrect)
- I **have no** money. (Corrected)
- I **don't have** money. (Corrected)
- Because no one paid me this week, I don't have money. (Appropriate construction involving two negatives)

VERB USAGE

Some verbs are often misused even by educated people, especially the verbs *lie* and *lay, sit* and *set,* and *rise* and *raise.*

Principal Parts

Present Form	Past Form	Past Participle Form
lie	lay	lain
lay	laid	laid
sit	sat	sat
set	set	set
rise	rose	risen
raise	raised	raised

Meanings:

Lie means to recline or rest in prone position.
(This is not to be confused with the verb meaning to tell a lie.)
Lay means to put or place.
(This is not to be confused with a hen laying an egg.)
Sit means to rest on the buttocks.
Set means to put or place.
Rise means to get up or to ascend.
Raise means to lift.

Intransitive (No Object)	Transitive (With Object)
lie	lay
sit	set
rise	raise

- We **lay** in the bright sun yesterday.
- He **laid** the package on the floor.
- They will **sit** in their chair.
- Bill and Martha **set** the table.
- The temperature has **risen** ten degrees.
- I **raise** the window each morning.

PUNCTUATION

USE OF THE PERIOD

Use a period at the end of a statement.
- I ate my lunch.
- Go home.

Use a period after abbreviations.
- Mrs.
- a.m.
- on Main St.
- George Jones, Jr.
- Dr. Irene Westerly, Ph.D.
- etc.

Note that there are some exceptions to the above, such as USA, TX, or NBC.

Use a period after initials.
- J. R. Stewart

Periods are used after letters and numerals in an outline.
```
I.
   A.
   B.
      1.
      2.
II.
```

USE OF THE QUESTION MARK

Use a question mark after a direct question.
- Who lost a book?

Note that indirect questions do not have a question mark.
- Tom asked who had lost a book.

USE OF THE COMMA

Some writers erroneously believe that a comma is needed for each vocal pause. This is untrue. Study the following sections to help you determine appropriate places for commas.

Commas with Coordinating Conjunctions

Use a comma before a coordinating conjunction that joins main clauses.
- No one saw the prowler, but everyone was scared.
- Birds sing, cows moo, pigs squeal, and dogs bark.
- The men and women in our group laughed and cried during the movie. (Simple sentence with compound subjects and predicates—no comma needed)

Sometimes if the main clauses are very short, commas may be omitted.
- Birds sing and cows moo.

Commas with Items in a Series

Use a comma to set off each item in a series of three or more parallel words, phrases, or clauses.
- The room was cold, dark, and dismal.
- The boys were strong, tall, little league players. (No comma after *little* because *little league* together modify players.)
- Turn off the lights, close the door, and leave the room.
- Dad's route goes to Washington or Oregon or California. (No comma is used when *and* or *or* are between all items.)

Commas with Introductory Elements

Use a comma after an introductory adverbial clause.
- If you leave soon, Phillip will be very sad.
- Before the next storm, we should get more wood for a fire.

If the introductory adverbial clause is very short, a comma will not be needed if the meaning is still clear.
- If he stays I'll be happy.

Use a comma after one or more introductory prepositional phrases with seven or more words.
- Early in the morning before the daybreak, Jim takes a walk.

Do not use the number seven rigidly. There are occasions when commas are needed although the words in this introductory element are fewer than seven. These commas aid in the understanding of the intended meaning.
- During the next dance, class members refused to participate.

Use a comma after introductory participial phrases.
- Squirting an offensive scent, the skunk paraded across the yard.

Use a comma after mild interjections.
- Oh, I forgot.
- Sh-h-h, the baby is sleeping.

Use a comma after introductory words such as *yes* and *no.*
- Yes, we will go.
- No, I prefer not to smoke.

Use a comma to separate words in direct address from the rest of the sentence.
- John, will you close the door?

GA1497

- Will you, John, close the door?
- Will you close the door, John?

Setting Off Selected Elements

Use a comma to set off each item in a date after the first item.
- On Wednesday, May 12, 1995, I learned how to type.
- My mother came to America in November 1944. (Commas are not used when the day of the week or the day of the month is omitted.)

Use a comma to set off each item in an address after the first item.
- My new address is Route 2, Box 590, Johnson City, Tennessee 37601. (No comma needed before the zip code.)
- Columbus, Ohio, is sometimes confused with Columbia, South Carolina.

Use a comma to separate two words or figures that might otherwise lead to confusion.
- At 10:42, 1,022 letters will be mailed.
- Our teacher requested that we march in, in order.

Use a comma to set off nonrestrictive (unneeded) phrases or clauses. A restrictive phrase or clause is <u>needed</u> to modify or identify a word in a sentence. A nonrestrictive phrase or clause usually adds unnecessary information to a sentence.
- My neighbor, who constantly eats junk food, is going with us to New Mexico. (Nonrestrictive clause)
- The ancient storyteller, strutting wildly in the tent, told one of my favorite tales. (Nonrestrictive phrase)
- My neighbor who constantly eats junk food has just learned he has an ulcer. (Restrictive clause)
- A boy who is captain of the football team was elected class president. (Restrictive clause)
- The ancient storyteller strutting wildly in the tent stumbled over the electrical wiring. (Restrictive participial phrase)
- Mary, my sister, is engaged. (Nonrestrictive appositive)
- I talked with Ned Turner, MD. (Abbreviations after names are nonrestrictive appositives, therefore requiring a comma.)
- My sister Mary is engaged. (Restrictive appositive. A comma is generally not used if the appositive is a proper noun.)
- Your new friend Ellen has just arrived. (Restrictive appositive)
- The word *separate* is frequently misspelled. (Restrictive appositive)

Use a comma to separate contrasted elements.
- Her words faded into the air, but not her fear.
- The basketball team, unlike the 4-H Club, uses the bus for its trips.

Use a comma to set off parenthetical words, phrases, and clauses. Examples of these expressions are as follows: *I think, I believe, I suppose, in my opinion, on the contrary, by the way, for example, however, to be sure, to tell the truth,* and *on the other hand.*
- Henri, in my most humble opinion, is the handsomest man in the village.
- No one, as you likely already know, should attempt this without training.

Do not use a comma to set off words such as *also, too, of course, perhaps, at least, therefore,* and *likewise* when they cause almost no pause in reading.
- I also would enjoy an expensive vacation.
- Cinderella was therefore freed from her dismal existence.

Use a comma to set off direct quotations from explanatory expressions.
- Mother shouted, "Who's at the door?"
- "What do you want," she inquired, "with such a tiny little cat?"

Use a comma to assist ease in reading.
- Before long, socks were his next purchase.
- Just the night before, Barbara had given him five dollars.

USE OF THE APOSTROPHE

Use an apostrophe to indicate the possessive case of nouns and indefinite pronouns.
- It was anyone's guess.
- The girl's father arrived. (Indicates the father of one girl)
- The girls' father arrived. (Indicates the father of more than one girl)
- That car of Joe's was a wreck.
- Scott and Betty's possessions were lost in the fire. (Indicates joint ownership of the possessions)
- Scott's and Betty's possessions were lost in the fire. (Indicates separate ownership)

Add an apostrophe and an *s* to plural nouns not ending in *s*.
- The women's division was closed.
- We toured the children's new playground.

Add only an apostrophe to plural nouns ending in *s*.
- The boys' bicycles were stolen.
- I ordered five dollars' worth of candy.

Use an apostrophe to mark the omitted letters in contractions.
- She'll not hear the crowd's applause before ten o'clock if she doesn't hurry.

The apostrophe often forms plurals of letters, figures, and words referred to as words.
- My e's and i's look alike.
- She made seven A's on her report card.

The apostrophe is not needed to form some plurals.
- In the 1900s there were no VFWs.

USE OF DOUBLE QUOTATION MARKS

Use double quotation marks to enclose material that is directly quoted.
- Mr. Smith said, "The money was in the vault."
- Mr. Smith said that the money was in the vault. (No quotation marks are used because there are no words that are directly quoted. This is called an indirect quote.)

Note that what each separate person says generally begins a new paragraph. All quoted material must appear exactly and cannot be changed. If paraphrasing occurs, the words may not appear in quotes.

If more than one paragraph by the same individual is quoted, use the beginning quotes for every paragraph, but use ending quotes for the last paragraph only.

Use double quotation marks to enclose borrowed words or phrases, words used in a very special way, or some slang expressions.
- He was considered a "dweeb" by his classmates.
- The entire gang was imprisoned for selling "smack."

Use double quotation marks to enclose titles of short poems, short stories, articles, lectures, chapters of books, songs, and short musical compositions.
- I have just read Joyce Kilmer's "Trees."
- Shel Silverstein's "Smart" is a poem about coins.
- The third chapter is entitled "The Black Spot."
- Marty sang "America the Beautiful" for her children.
- I called my lecture "The Return of Youth."

Note a designated order of punctuation marks when more than one occur together.
- "Hello," whispered the young maiden. (The comma precedes the quotation marks.)
- I had never before been called "special," but I liked the sound of it. (The comma precedes the quotation marks.)

GA1497

A semicolon will usually follow the quotation marks.
- No one read "Dark at Midnight"; all of the copies had disappeared.

The dash, question mark, and the exclamation point appear before the quotation marks when they refer to the quoted matter only; they follow when they refer to the whole sentence.
- He asked, "When did you leave?"
- What is the meaning of "fanazziba"?
- The guide screamed, "Run!"
- We'll not tolerate such "mercy"!

USE OF THE EXCLAMATION POINT

Use an exclamation point after a statement or an interjection showing surprise or strong feeling.
- What!
- Rush to the barn!
- Ouch! That hurts!
- No! Don't open that package!

USE OF THE HYPHEN

Use a hyphen to indicate end-of-the-line division.
- pre-
  pared
- mis-
  took

Use a hyphen between some prefix and root combinations, especially if the absence of the hyphen could cause confusion.
- pre-Renaissance
- re-cover a chair, but recover from an ailment

Use a hyphen in some compounds, particularly ones containing prepositions.
- The vice president-elect will visit our school next month.
- One day I will have a sister-in-law.
- She is a know-it-all snob.
- The sixth-grade student used the X-ray machine.
- The sixth grader had an X ray. (Note that the hyphen is used in these cases only when the phrase is used as an adjective.)

Use a hyphen with a several-word modifier when its use will help avoid confusion.
- Roger is a small-business man.
- I noticed his what-do-you-want look.

Sometimes hyphens will need to be suspended.
- She collected the sixth- and eighth-grade student fees.
- We will compare the pre- and post-test results very soon.

Use a hyphen when writing out compound numbers between 21 and 99.
- I read seventy-eight books in one hundred thirty-two days.
- There have been fifty-three accidents on that street.

Use a hyphen with some fractions.
- A two-thirds vote produced an upset for one third of the members. (Notice that the hyphen is used when the expression is an adjective.)

Use a hyphen with some figures or letters.
- The poem is on pages 28-41.
- During the 1996-1999 years, my zip code will be 76192-0041, and my telephone number will be (616) 442-9618.
- The mid-1980s produced some colorful and unusual T-shirts.

Use the hyphen to compound capitalized names.
- The Denver-San Francisco flight contained some anti-American passengers.

USE OF THE COLON

Use a colon between the hour and the minute in a time statement.
- We arrived at 12:47.

- No lunch will be served before 12:00.

Use a colon after the salutation in business letters.
- Dear Sir:
- Gentlemen:

Use a colon to draw attention to what follows and for other special instances.
- I wanted only one thing: freedom.
- To complete this task you will need the following items: a flashlight, a drinking straw, and an envelope.
- The man quoted Genesis 4:24.

USE OF THE SEMICOLON

Use a semicolon between two main clauses not joined by a conjunction in a compound sentence.
- Jack likes basketball; George detests it.
- Samuel watched the shadow disappear, started his hike, and walked to the river; he was in pain no more.

A semicolon is frequently (but not always) used between two main clauses joined by a conjunction in a compound sentence containing one or more commas.
- Mr. Simpson, the tennis coach, brought the players, parents, and sponsors; but no one brought the principal.

A semicolon is frequently (but not always) used between two main clauses in a complex sentence containing a comma.
- The school nurse, who is my next-door neighbor, spoke to our class; but she arrived very late.

Use a semicolon before conjunctive adverbs and transitional phrases connecting main clauses. The following are examples of conjunctive adverbs: *however, therefore, also, consequently, moreover, besides,* and *then.*
- Marie became a cheerleader in her sophomore year; moreover, she was elected captain in her senior year.
- Bruce was on the football team in the spring; however, he was soon injured.

USE OF SINGLE QUOTATION MARKS

Use single quotation marks to enclose a quotation or a title within a quotation.
- The reporter said, "My mother used the expression, 'Don't buy a pig in a poke,' but I don't know what it means."
- "Each day I read a verse of 'Good Morning to You' before I eat breakfast," the man told his boss.

USE OF PARENTHESES

Use parentheses to set off some supplementary, parenthetical, or explanatory material.
- My first three classes (all at a different school) were quite successful.
- Ted hopes (as I do) that a solution can be reached soon.
- The music stopped (no one knows why) before the man entered.

Use parentheses to enclose Arabic numerals that confirm a written number in a text.
- Delivery will be made in sixty (60) days.

Use parentheses to enclose numbers or letters in a series.
- The three things needed are as follows: (1) the class roll, (2) the permission forms, and (3) the driver's insurance papers.

USE OF THE DASH

Use a dash to indicate an abrupt change or break in the sentence.
- I tied the shoelaces together—no one noticed—before he awakened.

Use a dash after an introductory series of items.
- Milk, flour, and eggs—these are the ingredients all our recipes will require.

GA1497

The dash often precedes the attribution of a quotation.
- How lucky to be me . . . . —George Steiner

USE OF THE BRACKETS

Use brackets to set off extraneous data such as editorial interpolations especially within quoted material.
- He wrote, "I recieved [sic] your letter."

Use brackets to set off material within parentheses.
- Please read Chapter 12 (Paragraph 4 [including the next four sentences] and Paragraph 10).

CAPITALIZATION

Capitalize the first word in a sentence or sentence fragment.
- Sunshine helps warm my spirit.
- How do you do?
- Wow!
- He replied, "We can stay only a few minutes."

Always capitalize the pronoun I.
- She and I are best friends!

Capitalize the first word in a direct quotation.
- Sean shouted, "Run to the shelter!"
- After a long while he sighed, "Yes, I'll stay."

Capitalize the specific names of persons and places.
- George Washington
- Michael Jordan
- California
- Elm Street
- Carter Boulevard
- Grand Canyon
- Mississippi River

Capitalize some abbreviations.
- . . . in Reno, NV
- . . . to Mr. and Mrs. Lee . . .
- . . . while watching TV in his room . . .
- . . . the IRS . . .

Capitalize some initials.
- . . . addressed to B. J. Scott

Capitalize the the names of school subjects that are language studies.
- . . . enrolled in Spanish II . . .
- . . . in the English workbook . . .

Capitalize the brand names of some products.
- Chef Boyardee pizza mix
- Campbell's soup
- Lipton tea

Capitalize the specific names of organizations and their members.
- Rotary International
- Kiwanians
- Yale University
- Federal Express
- Democratic party
- the Atomic Energy Commission

Capitalize the specific names of historical documents, periods, and events.
- the Bill of Rights
- the Fifth Amendment
- the Middle Ages
- Vietnam War

Capitalize words indicating family relatives when these words precede the name of a person.
- Uncle Jim
- Aunt Irene
- Cousin Steve
- Grandpa Sanders

Capitalize the first word of the greeting in a letter and the first word of the complimentary close.
- Dear Mr. Evans
- My dear Aunt Mrytle
- Sincerely yours
- Yours sincerely

Capitalize the days of the week, the months of the year.
- Saturday
- September

Do not capitalize the seasons of the year.
- spring
- winter

Capitalize holidays and holy days.
- Thanksgiving
- Martin Luther King, Jr. Day
- Halloween
- Labor Day

In titles capitalize the first and last words and all other words except prepositions, articles, and short conjunctions.
- *Gone with the Wind*
- "The Wolf and the Seven Little Goats"
- "My Bonnie Lies over the Ocean"

Capitalize words designating peoples and languages.
- Canadians
- Hispanics
- Latin
- French
- Cherokee

Capitalize words derived from proper names.
- Americanize (used as a verb)
- Roman numerals
- Shakespearean comedies
- pro-American ways

Capitalize titles preceding the name of a person but not those that follow it.
- President Clinton
- Rex Shields, our governor
- Professor Elliott
- Pope Paul
- Queen Elizabeth

Capitalize words designating the Deity and pronouns referring to the Deity.
- the Lord, Himself

Capitalize the first word of a direct question within a sentence.
- The question was posed: Which came first, the chicken or the egg?

Capitalize the first word of most lines of poetry.
- Little Jack Horner
- Sat in a corner . . .

Capitalize the names of ships, aircraft, and spacecraft.
- The Good Ship Hollyhock
- *Apollo 13*

Capitalize the names of specific courts of law.
- the Circuit Court of the United States
- the Utah Court of Appeals

Capitalize planets, constellations, stars, and groups of stars. Generally, the sun and moon are not capitalized.
- Pluto
- Little Dipper
- Sirius

GA1497